THE BRIDGESTONE
100 BEST PLACES TO STAY IN IRELAND 200

GW00326351

THE BRIDGESTONE

100 BEST
PLACES TO STAY
IN IRELAND 2003

JOHN McKENNA - SALLY McKENNA

ESTRAGON PRESS

FIRST PUBLISHED IN 2003

BY ESTRAGON PRESS

DURRUS

COUNTY CORK

© ESTRAGON PRESS

TEXT © JOHN & SALLY McKENNA

THE MORAL RIGHT OF THE AUTHORS HAS

BEEN ASSERTED

ISBN 1 874076 46 4

PRINTED IN SPAIN BY GRAPHYCEMS

WRITTEN BY JOHN McKENNA

CONTRIBUTING EDITORS:

ORLA BRODERICK

ELIZABETH FIELD

CLAIRE GOODWILLIE

CAROLINE WORKMAN

PUBLISHING EDITOR: SALLY McKENNA

EDITOR: JUDITH CASEY

ART DIRECTION BY NICK CANN

COVER PHOTOS BY MIKE O'TOOLE

ILLUSTRATIONS BY AOIFE WASSER

WEB: FLUIDEDGE.IE

WEB CONTRIBUTING EDITOR: LESLIE WILLIAMS

FOR PETER WARD

WITH THANKS TO...

Colm Conyngham, Des Collins, Brian Condon,

Frieda Forde, Sile Ginnane, Conor Cahill,

Judith Casey,

Nick Cann, Pat Young,

Margie Deverell, Lelia McKenna,

Mike O'Toole, Ann Marie Tobin,

Josette Cadoret,

Hugh Stancliffe,

Mark & Millie Deverell

Bridgestone is the world's largest tyre and rubber company.

■ Founded in Japan in 1931, it currently employs over 100,000 people in Europe, Asia and America and its products are sold in more than 150 countries. Its European plants are situated in France, Spain, Italy, Poland and Turkey.

■ Bridgestone manufacture tyres for a wide variety of vehicles from passenger cars and motorcycles, trucks and buses to giant earthmovers and aircraft.

■ Many new cars are fitted with Bridgestone tyres during manufacture including Ford, Toyota, Volkswagen, Mercedes and BMW. Ferrari and Porsche are also fitted with Bridgestone performance tyres as original equipment.

■ Bridgestone commercial vehicle tyres enjoy a worldwide reputation for durability and its aircraft tyres are used by more than 100 airlines.

■ In Formula 1 Bridgestone supply tyres to leading teams and drivers, including Ferrari and Michael Schumacher. Technology developed in the sport has lead to increased performance and safety in Bridgestone's road tyres.

■ Bridgestone tyres are distributed in Ireland by Bridgestone Ireland Ltd, a subsidiary of the multinational Bridgestone Corporation. A wide range of tyres are stocked in its 70,000 square foot central warehouse and its staff provide sales, technical and delivery services all over Ireland.

■ Bridgestone tyres are available from First Stop Tyre Centres and tyre dealers throughout Ireland.

FOR FURTHER INFORMATION:

BRIDGESTONE IRELAND LTD
Balbriggan
Co Dublin
Tel: (01) 8415200
Fax: (01) 8415245

34 Hillsborough Road
Lisburn
BT28 1AQ
Tel: (028) 92678331

websites:
www.bridgestone-eu.com
www.firststop-eu.com

• The Irish have an old fashioned belief that hospitality is an instinct. It's not. Hospitality is an art form, and, like any art form, it demands the true grit of learning, application, study, tutoring and working alongside the best in the business in order to truly master the art. And there are few more demanding arts, few that ask so much of one's time, patience, and material and intellectual resources, as the Art of Hospitality.

• Allied to an instinct for looking after people, perfecting the art of hospitality breeds people who are superlatively good at the business of looking after other people. These are the very practitioners whom we have sought out for this book, those who know that instinct alone is not enough, those who keep on trying, perfecting, polishing.

• What we chase after, year in and year out, are people in whom the natural instinct and the practised artistry lead – almost inevitably – to originality. The very best people in this book have transcended our expectations, and emerged into a territory where they operate according to their own laws.

• Hospitality, design, ambience, feng shui, cooking, all flow according to their own will. This originality is thrilling – a pure thrill – and we hope this book allows you to find it.

John & Sally McKenna
Durrus, West Cork, February 2003

'The primary task of the critic... is the recreation of texture.. filing a sensory report on the experience'

– 'Nobody's Perfect' Anthony Lane

• We are always amazed – and amused – by those guide books that tell you the square footage of the conference centre in the Hotel de Luxe, or the precise length of the swimming pool which has been newly installed at a cost of a squillion euro in the Manoir aux Cinq Saisons.

• They are the same books which – diligently, we admit – advert to the availability of trouser presses and hairdryers, and whether or not the junior suite has a Jacuzzi bath. After all, who wants a junior suite that doesn't have a Jacuzzi bath?

• Such books do an undoubtedly important job, but they remind us of movie criticism – the business about which Anthony Lane is writing – which precis the storyline, give a nod to the director, opine that the actor has delivered a realistic portrayal, and which conclude by telling you that the movie was amongst the 'top grossers' in its opening weekend. Top grossers? Hmm.

• All that counts with movies can be summed up in one question: did they make the magic? And what will do for

an icon

a classic

worth a detour

a comfort zone

movies will do for hospitality, for all we want to know, whenever we are bidding our farewells and leaving a new place, is: did they make the magic?

• If they did, you will find them in these pages. If they did the magic big time, then you will find them laden down with awards. If they didn't, then you might find them in some other book, but you won't find them here.

• Trouser presses, junior Jacuzzi suites and all that stuff are for people who want to know the top grossers. What we want to describe is the texture – of the people, their house or hotel, their greeting, their care, their cooking – and how this texture converts into an experience which is pleasing to one's spirit. The reports which follow are sensory reports: what did it feel like?

icons

Assolas Country House, Kanturk

Ballymaloe House, Shanagarry

Buggy's Glencairn Inn, Glencairn

The Clarence, Dublin

Fortview House, Goleen

Kelly's Resort Hotel, Rosslare

Longueville House, Mallow

The Mustard Seed, Echo Lodge, Ballingarry

Newport House, Newport

Norman Villa, Galway

The Quay House, Clifden

Richmond House, Cappoquin

Salville House, Enniscorthy

Shelburne Lodge, Kenmare

Temple House, Ballymote

classic

Ballynahinch Castle, Recess

Ballyvolane House, Fermoy

Blindgate House, Kinsale

Glenally House, Youghal

Iskeroon, Caherdaniel

Kilgraney Country House, Bagenalstown

Killarney Park Hotel, Killarney

The Moat Inn, Templepatrick

The Morrison, Dublin

Number 31, Dublin

The Park Hotel, Kenmare

Rathcoursey House, Midleton

Zuni, Kilkenny

detour

Clifden House, Corofin

Dolphin Beach, Clifden

Ghan House, Carlingford

Hilton Park, Clones

Marble Hall, Dublin

Sea Mist, Clifden

Sheen Falls Lodge, Kenmare

comfort zone

Ballyknocken House, Ashford

Beech Hill Country House, Craigantlet

Bow Hall, Castletownsend

Devon Dell, Galway

Hanora's Cottage, Nire Valley

The Hibernian Hotel, Dublin

• The Bridgestone 100 Best Places to Stay in Ireland is arranged **ALPHABETICALLY, BY COUNTY** so it begins with County Carlow, which is followed by County Cavan, and so on.

• Within the counties, the entries are once again listed alphabetically, so Aherne's, in Youghal, East Cork, is followed by Assolas House, in Kanturk, North Cork.

• Entries in Northern Ireland are itemised alphabetically, at the end of the book. All NI prices quoted in sterling.

• The contents of the Bridgestone 100 Best Guides are exclusively the result of the authors' deliberations. All meals and accommodation were paid for and any offers of discounts or gifts were refused.

• Many of the places featured in this book are only open during the summer season, which means that they can be closed for any given length of time between October and March. Many others change their opening times during the winter.

• **PRICES:** Average prices are calculated on the basis of one night's stay for bed and breakfast. Look out for special offers for weekends, several days' stay, or off season.

• **CREDIT CARDS:** Most houses take major credit cards, particularly the Visa, Access/Master group. Check if you intend to use American Express or Diners Card. If a house does not accept credit cards, this is indicated in the notes section of their entry.

• Finally, we greatly appreciate receiving reports, suggestions and criticisms from readers, and would like to thank those who have written in the past, whose opinions are of enormous assistance to us when considering which 100 places to stay finally make it into this book.

CONTENTS

BARROWVILLE TOWNHOUSE

Randal & Marie Dempsey
Kilkenny Road
Carlow, County Carlow
Tel: (059) 914 3324
Fax: 914 1953
www.barrowvillehouse.com

Meticulous and painstaking attention to every detail is the characteristic of Randal and Marie Dempsey's elegant, hospitable Barrowville Townhouse.

The Carlow region offers some of the most charming and unspoilt scenery and small towns and villages to be found in Ireland. Yet, for many, it remains a place simply to pass through, as you head on to destinations such as Kilkenny or further south. This may yet prove to be the salvation of the place: the Carlow region only needs to be overlooked for another little while, and then, like West Waterford, it will suddenly be discovered, unspoilt. And, then, we shall be grateful to pioneering professionals like Randal and Marie Dempsey, people who have been creating the template for high standards, swish style, good hospitality and excellent cooking, all of which they exhibit in the elegant Barrowville townhouse. This is a great base for exploring, but it's also a great place to escape to, a place to chill out, a place to get the measure of this lovely, undiscovered, gentle, quiet area.

- **OPEN:** All year
- **ROOMS:** Seven rooms, all en suite
- **PRICE:** €75.75 per double room, single room €50.50, B&B

- **NOTES:**
Visa, Master, Amex. No dinner. No wheelchair access. Private car parking.
Children over 12 years welcome.

- **DIRECTIONS:**
On the right hand side after the traffic lights heading south out of Carlow. 50 miles from Dublin (Route N9); 50 miles from Rosslare (again N9).

KILGRANEY COUNTRY HOUSE

Bryan Leech & Martin Marley
Bagenalstown
County Carlow
Tel: (059) 977 5283 Fax: 977 5595
info@kilgraneyhouse.com
www.kilgraneyhouse.com

north

east

west

south

The new outhouses promise
to make Bryan and Martin's
Kilgraney one of the key
destinations of the decade.

As the developments of the outhouses and out buildings
continue apace at Kilgraney, one can see the steady
emergence of what promises to be one of the major
destination resorts of the decade. A series of self-catering
cottages and apartments will form a perfect counterpoint
to the elegant old house itself, and for Dubliners, in
particular, escaping to this 'sunny wood', between
Bagenalstown and Borris, is likely to become an addiction.
Mind you, there will be many others who simply won't
relinquish their need to have a fix of this gorgeous,
provocative house, and the superb hospitality and
cooking of Martin and Bryan. Everything about Kilgraney
is cult: the style, the decoration, the wit, the sheer élan
with which this talented pair have graced the house.
Already, the same keen eye can be seen in the design of
the revamped buildings: style lovers can expect the best.

- **OPEN:** Mar-Nov weekends, Jul-Aug weekly
- **ROOMS:** Six double, en suite rooms
- **PRICE:** €45-€85 per person sharing, €90-€170
room rate. Weekend packages available.

- **NOTES:**
Visa, Master, Amex, Laser. Dinner 8pm €40, communal
table, book by noon. Wheelchair access with assistance.
Enclosed car park. Children 0-12yrs by arrangement only.

- **DIRECTIONS:**
Just off the R705, 3.5 miles from Bagenalstown (Muine
Bheag) on the road heading towards Borris. Dublin
Airport 75 miles. Rosslare Ferry Port 55 miles.

LORD BAGENAL INN

James & Mary Kehoe
Leighlinbridge, County Carlow
Tel: (0503) 21668
Fax: (0503) 22629
info@lordbagenal.com
www.lordbagenal.com

Colour is the key to Leighlinbridge: the flowers on the streets during the season, and the vivid plash of colour in James Kehoe's great art collection.

It must be something in the air, or the water. Whatever it is, the good people of Leighlinbridge ('Locklin'', as they call it) are obsessed with colour, specifically the Monet-like shimmer of colour from the multitude of flowers with which they bedeck the village during the Entente Floriale, a competition they take very seriously indeed.

How fitting, then, that James Kehoe, boss of the Lord Bagenal, should also be obsessed with colour, though in Mr Kehoe's case it is the vivid colour of modern abstract art which covets his time, and his money. Mr Kehoe has assembled one of the very best collections of modern art you can enjoy, and he hangs it throughout this lovely restaurant and bar in order that we can all enjoy it. It is just one feature of an address which improves every year, year in and year out, a lovely place to escape to, a great place to eat, an incalculably valuable asset to the village.

- **OPEN:** All year, except Christmas Day
- **ROOMS:** 12 en suite bedrooms
- **PRICE:** €55 midweek, €62.50 Fri/Sat per person sharing, single supplement €25 for bed and breakfast

- **NOTES:**
Carvery lunch. Afternoon bar menu. Evening bar menu from 6pm. Dinner from €35. Limited wheelchair access. Private parking. Children welcome, playroom, babysitting.

- **DIRECTIONS:**
8 miles south of Carlow, signed off the main N9 Dublin/Kilkenny route. 20 miles north of Kilkenny.

MacNEAN HOUSE

The Maguire family
Blacklion
County Cavan
Tel: (072) 53022
Fax: (072) 53404

The modest little MacNean is the prototype food lovers destination, and it's packed every weekend with people who travel from far for great cooking.

Neven Maguire's extraordinary cooking has created one of the most resoundingly successful food lover's pilgrimage destinations in Ireland. Every weekend, not only the five rooms of the MacNean itself, but also two other local B&B's, are packed with food lovers who have made their merry way up to little Blacklion, thrilled with the prospect before them, sated with delight as they head back on Sunday after a couple of days feasting on Mr Maguire's meticulous, exciting, creative cooking.

To have created such a destination address is no small achievement, for the MacNean is modest, the rooms unremarkable. And yet, they chime perfectly with the modest, hard-working, quiet country métier which animates this happy house. The MacNean is a prototype for how great cooking can attract outsiders to a region: as with so many other things, Neven Maguire is a pioneer.

- **OPEN:** All year, except Christmas
- **ROOMS:** Five rooms
- **PRICE:** €30-€35 per person sharing

- **NOTES:**
Visa, Mastercard.
MacNean Bistro opens for Dinner, €55
Wheelchair access.
Children welcome.
Recommended for vegetarians.

- **DIRECTIONS:**
On the main street in Blacklion, which itself is just on the border with Northern Ireland.

CLIFDEN HOUSE

Jim & Bernadette Robson
Corofin, County Clare
Tel: (065) 6837692
Fax: 6837692
www.clifdenhouse-countyclare.ie
clifdenhousecountyclare@eircom.net

Debonair and raffish, and
deliriously good fun:
that's the unique Clifden
House prescription.

'Debonair' is the term that always comes to mind when
you think about Clifden House and its owners and
keepers, Jim and Bernadette Robson.

It's slightly raffish, in the most charmingly down-at-heel
way, and that faded gentility, that smiling charm, animates
a handsome old house which the Robsons struggle to
keep together and steadily improve and colonise. It is a
lifetime's work, and a task which they go about with pluck
and good cheer, ladling their work with their own charm
and insouciance. It all makes sense when you have a
gaggle of dinner guests arrayed around the big table in the
dining room, and when conversation and good cheer are
sparked, and it gets into overdrive when Jim joins the
table and starts to tell his charming tales with the
seasoned wit of the natural raconteur. You feel, then, that
you have moved back in time, to a gentler, easier place.

- **OPEN:** Mar-end Oct
- **ROOMS:** Five rooms
- **PRICE:** €65 per person sharing, €90 single

- **NOTES:**
Visa, Mastercard. Dinner, 8pm, €35, communal table.
Private car parking. Two self-catering houses in
courtyard, sleeps 6 or 8. Priced weekly. Children
welcome. Two boats for guest use.

- **DIRECTIONS:**
Left of the grotto in the village, second right, then first
right into the drive. Limerick-Ennis on N18, turn onto
coast road. 1 hour from Galway or Limerick.

FERGUS VIEW

Mary Kelleher
Kilnaboy, Corofin
County Clare
Tel: (065) 683 7606
Fax: 683 7192
deckell@indigo.ie

There is something elemental and pleasing about a cosy B&B such as Mary Kelleher's little Fergus View, an archetype of the real country B&B.

The best places to stay fit into our psyche as neatly as we fit into their comfy chairs and swaddlesome beds, and so it is with Fergus View. Mary Kelleher's B&B is simple, straightforward, unpretentious, but the warmth of the welcome, the quality of the hospitality, the eagerness of the cooking and the comforting nature of the house all combine to make it quite irresistible.

Mrs Kelleher does everything well, from tasty breakfasts that show real care in the cooking, meticulous housekeeping that delights the eye, and lovely, domestic dinners that fizzle with the flavours of a good country cook. All in all, Fergus View makes complete sense as a place to base yourself if exploring the flora of the Burren, a house which you will leave with a contented tum in the morning, and to which you will be looking forward to returning in the evening for a soulful, scrummy dinner.

- **OPEN:** Easter-mid Oct
- **ROOMS:** Six rooms, five en suite
- **PRICE:** €33 per person sharing. Single room €46-€48

- **NOTES:**
No credit cards. Dinner Mon-Thur if pre booked.
No dinners Fri-Sun or bank hols. Dinner €23.50.
No wheelchair access.
Secure parking. Children welcome.

- **DIRECTIONS:**
From Ennis take the main road to Ennistymon but turn off to the right for Corofin after one mile. It is 2 miles north of Corofin on the road to Kilfenora.

MOY HOUSE

Antoin O'Looney
Lahinch
County Clare
Tel: (065) 708 2800 Fax: 708 2500
moyhouse@eircom.net
www.moyhouse.com

Hitchcock fans take note: Moy House has a bell tower straight out of the master's movie, 'Vertigo'. But, nothing scary about the rest of this fine house.

An architecturally fascinating mid-19th century house with a tower, which looks out on the majestic Liscannor Bay from its hill perch, just south of Lahinch, Moy House is managed by Bernie Merry. And there is no one better – or better named – than Ms Merry to make you feel a million dollars as you enjoy a few days in this fine house. But, make sure you get the right rooms: these are the rooms on the first floor which have sea views, and they are the ones to chase, for to watch the light die over Liscannor Bay in the evening is some sort of bliss. Mind you, you may only have eyes for the comfy big beds, and the excellently equipped bathrooms, which are truly special. The cooking is imaginative – Burren Smokehouse salmon; local lamb, eggs Benedict in the morning – and will likely continue to improve. But Moy is a house slowly coming into its own, thanks to the splendid Ms Merry.

- **OPEN:** Mid Jan-end Dec
- **ROOMS:** Nine rooms
- **PRICE:** €97.50-€114.50 per person sharing

- **NOTES:**
All major cards accepted.
Special offers Nov-May.
Group rates accepted.
Dinner €45.

- **DIRECTIONS:**
Moy House is located about one mile out of Lahinch town, on the Miltown Malbay road. Shannon airport is 1 hour's drive.

AHERNE'S

The Fitzgibbon family
163 North Main Street
Youghal, East Cork
Tel: (024) 92424, Fax: 93633
ahernes@eircom.net
www.ahernes.com

The secret of Aherne's is pretty simple: the Fitzgibbon family have good taste, and they put it to work in every aspect of their establishment.

They are building a by-pass road around Youghal. Are they crazy? What sensible, food-loving traveller is going to detour around the town when Aherne's is there in the centre, beckoning you with its delicious food in both the bar and the restaurant, and its comfortable, spacious rooms a beacon of light for the tired traveller who wants to find some solace from the road. By-pass the town? Are they crazy?

Aherne's is tasteful in every way, from the super-efficient and personable service, to the delicious cooking, to the smart, stylish rooms. It is one of those addresses that works with ruthless efficiency and self-discipline to keep itself up to the mark, which means that Aherne's never dates, never goes out of fashion, remains always at the cutting edge. It is not just a staple of the Bridgestone guides, but a staple of the best kind of Irish hospitality.

- **OPEN:** All year
- **ROOMS:** 12 rooms, all en suite
- **PRICE:** €70-€105 p.p.s. Single €110 (single supplement of €40 single occupancy of junior suite)

- **NOTES:**
Children welcome, 5-12yrs 50% reduction if sharing. Full wheelchair access. Secure parking.

- **DIRECTIONS:**
Youghal is on a one-way system, coming from Cork direction: when you get back onto the two-way system Aherne's Seafood Restaurant & Hotel is located 50 yards on the right-hand side – a yellow building.

10 PLACES WITH
GREAT BREAKFASTS

AN BOHREEN
DUNGARVAN, Co WATERFORD

BALLYKNOCKEN HOUSE
ASHFORD, Co WICKLOW

THE CLARENCE
DUBLIN, Co DUBLIN

HANORA'S COTTAGE
NIRE VALLEY, Co WATERFORD

MADDYBENNY FARM HOUSE
PORTRUSH, Co ANTRIM

MARBLE HALL
DUBLIN, Co DUBLIN

NEWPORT HOUSE
NEWPORT, Co MAYO

THE OLD WORKHOUSE
DUNSHAUGHLIN, Co MEATH

POWERSFIELD HOUSE
DUNGARVAN, Co WATERFORD

SHELBURNE LODGE
KENMARE, Co KERRY

ASSOLAS COUNTRY HOUSE

Joe & Hazel Bourke
Kanturk
North Cork
Tel: (029) 50015 Fax: 50795
assolas@eircom.net
www.assolas.com

Assolas is one of the greatest country houses, with unique, profound cooking and a sublime, gentle ambience.

'The food was the ultimate demonstration of how to cook the very best ingredients in a simple way.' That's as sharp and succinct a summation of Hazel Bourke's glorious cooking as you will come across, courtesy of a 'food loving' Bridgestone reader, and along with 'simple' and 'very best', the key word here is really 'ultimate'. Hazel Bourke's cooking really does reach a pinnacle, of flavour, texture, composition, irrespective of what it is that she is cooking. Every ingredient falls under her spell, from her trademark pan haggerty to subtle meat and shellfish cookery, and what a mighty spell. Not to be left behind, Joe Bourke runs this gorgeous house with as much command as his wife demonstrates in the kitchen, and together they are a mighty team, creating a gentle vibe that makes a stay in this gorgeous house nothing less than an enchantment: Assolas really is the ultimate.

- **OPEN:** Mid Mar-Nov
- **ROOMS:** Six rooms, all en suite
- **PRICE:** B&B €85-€126 per person sharing.

- Dinner 7pm-8pm, €48. Vegetarian and special diets welcome with notice. No wheelchair access.
Private car park.
Children welcome, under 5s sharing, free. Garden for children to play in.

- **DIRECTIONS:**
Take the N72 Mallow/Killarney road, and 10km west of Mallow you will see the first signpost. 33 miles from Cork airport (approx 1 hour).

BALLYMALOE HOUSE

The Allen family
Shanagarry
Midleton, East Cork
Tel: (021) 465 253, Fax: 465 2029
res@ballymaloe.ie
www.ballymaloe.com

Ballymaloe House is modest, gracious, timeless, and a place which is simply, irrevocably, unforgettable: unique.

It still surprises some folk, when they arrive at Ballymaloe House for the very first time, to realise just how simple – how small! – this legendary country house actually is. Indeed, there is nothing grand about Ballymaloe: grandness, in fact, would be antithetical to the quiet, Quakerish nature of the Allen family.

But Ballymaloe makes its presence felt in the most profound way. It never leaves you, in fact, once you have stayed here for a few days. We can still recall every detail of our first ever visit – we arrived on bicycles! – we still remember the sight of Myrtle Allen clearing a table late on that Saturday night, still recall the gorgeous food and wines, that perfect piece of Milleens, that stroll in the grounds after dinner, breakfast in bed the next morning. That experience has never left us, and that is why Ballymaloe is world famous: it is an unforgettable house.

- **OPEN:** All year
- **ROOMS:** 34 rooms. No suites
- **PRICE:** €95-€140 per person sharing.
Single supplement €25

- **NOTES:**
All major credit cards accepted. Dinner 7pm-9.30pm, €55. Recommended for vegetarians. Children welcome, cot, high chair, early dinner. Private parking.

- **DIRECTIONS:**
18 miles east of Cork city. Take N25 to exit for Whitegate R630, follow signs for R629 Cloyne. House is 2 miles beyond Cloyne.

BALLYVOLANE HOUSE

Merrie & Jeremy Green
Castlelyons
Fermoy, North Cork
Tel: (025) 36349, Fax: 36781
ballyvol@iol.ie
www.ballyvolanehouse.ie

Ballyvolane is one of the great country houses, and offers one of the great country house experiences.

Ballyvolane is one of the great country houses, and offers one of the great country house experiences. Pitch up here – it's best to take the last turning off the N8 after you have passed through Rathcormac, going south – and you enter a little fairy tale of good living, a dream detour away from reality and the modern world as we know it. But Ballyvolane works so well, and creates such an enchantment, precisely because Merrie and Jeremy work so hard. The attention to detail in Ballyvolane – every detail – is simply fantastic, in particular the care taken with the cooking, which produces some of the best country house cooking in Ireland. This excellent food, and the round-the-table bonhommie it inspires amongst the contented guests, is the centrepiece of the Ballyvolane escape, a delicious note to this step out of reality and into a delightful, all-enveloping dreamscape.

- **OPEN:** 1 Jan-23 Dec
- **ROOMS:** Six rooms, all en suite
- **PRICE:** €65-€80 per person B&B

- **NOTES:**
Amex, Visa, Mastercard accepted. Dinner 8pm, €37, communal table.
Wheelchair access in one bedroom.
Private car park.
Children welcome, high chair, cot.

- **DIRECTIONS:**
From the N8, south just after Rathcormac, take the turn to Midleton and look for the sign for the house.

BARNABROW

Geraldine O'Brien
Cloyne, Midleton
East Cork
Tel: (021) 465 2534, Fax: 465 2534
barnabrow@eircom.net
www.barnabrowhouse.com

Barnabrow is almost a universe unto itself, a house which takes guests which also has a restaurant, organic garden, wildlife sanctuary and shop.

Geraldine O'Brien's stoic energy powers the lovely Barnabrow ever onwards. Style lovers crave this stylishly elegant house for its individuality and beauty, and indeed Mrs O'Brien has a meticulous eye for colour and furnishings, keeping Barnabrow right up there with all the other immensely stylish houses which are such a feature of East Cork (in design terms, East Cork equals the high standards which Kenmare boasts of in food terms or West Waterford enjoys in terms of hospitality: there is a little thesis lurking here for a design student).

But that is not all there is to this house, which also has a fine garden, an animal sanctuary, a shop selling African furniture, and which is also a key destination for locals holding weddings, who want a dreamily romantic place in which to celebrate in style. It's a little micro-universe, is Barnabrow, and more power to Mrs O'Brien's energy.

- **OPEN:** All year, except 24-28 Dec
- **ROOMS:** 19 en suite rooms
- **PRICE:** €50-€75 per person sharing, €13 single supplement.

- **NOTES:**
Restaurant serves dinner, 7pm-9pm, €38. Wheelchair access only with assistance. Secure parking. Children welcome - donkeys, goats, hens, ducks, geese.

- **DIRECTIONS:**
From N25 take Cloyne exit, turn left at Ballinacorra. Take Ballycotton road from Cloyne Cross, house is 2 miles out of village on left, before Ballymaloe House.

BLAIR'S COVE HOUSE

Philippe & Sabine de Mey
Durrus
Bantry
West Cork
Tel: (027) 61127, Fax: 61487
blairscove@eircom.net

An extraordinary location, gorgeous rooms, and a swooningly romantic restaurant room: that's the winning Blair's Cove West Cork recipe.

A friend described the dining room in Blair's Cove as being 'jaw dropping for those on a first visit'. That's absolutely true: it's a gorgeous, high-ceilinged temple for eating, and on a first visit the romance of the location – the house sits on a promontory reaching out into lovely Dunmanus Bay, just south of Durrus village on the road to Goleen – merely accentuates the stunning beauty of the whole experience.

Philippe and Sabine de Mey have the good sense, then, to ensure that the rooms which adjoin the house are just as gorgeous as the location and the restaurant. These are immensely stylish places to stay, with a glamour and tactility that makes them hard to leave, and their design is hugely welcoming and comforting. Do note that the apartments can be rented for self catering, should you be seeking a West Cork base for touring the peninsulas.

● **OPEN:** Mar-Nov
● **ROOMS:** three courtyard suites, one cottage in grounds
● **PRICE:** €85-€100 per person sharing. Single supplement €30

● **NOTES:**
All major cards accepted. Restaurant serves dinner, Tue-Sat, €48. Children welcome.
Self-catering cottage available.

● **DIRECTIONS:**
1.5km outside the village of Durrus on the Barleycove/Mizen Head road. Look for the blue gates.

BLINDGATE HOUSE

Maeve Coakley
Blindgate, Kinsale
West Cork
Tel: (021) 477 7858, Fax: 477 7868
info@blindgatehouse.com
www.blindgatehouse.com

The aesthetic details of the Vivienne Roche paintings in Blindgate are echoed by this lovely house.

'I like the old and the new, but I like simple,' says Teresa Coakley, and her beautiful house, Blindgate, is tribute to a woman who relishes the cleanness and comfort and timelessness of simple. Chic simple. Cook simple. Classic simple: Blindgate has them all in its marvellous weave of furnishings, fabrics, colours and contrasts. Indeed, one of the design features that adorns this house, the series of hotel paintings by Vivienne Roche, is a perfect summation of that simplicity: the paintings are all about very obvious architectural features, rendered with stunning clarity that says to you: look at this closely, look at this again, look at this closely again.

So it is with Blindgate. You have to look closely at the details here, because they are so winningly understated, so contemplative. It's a beautiful, enchanting house, with beautiful breakfasts cooked with relish and quiet aplomb.

● **OPEN:** Mar-Dec
● **ROOMS:** 11 rooms (seven twin rooms, three standard double rooms & one superior double)
● **PRICE:** €125-€160 per room

● **NOTES:**
Visa, Mastercard, Amex. No dinner. Wheelchair access with assistance, but no walk-in showers. Ample enclosed parking. No children under 8 years.

● **DIRECTIONS:**
From Dublin road, notice Supervalu on right. Keep straight rather than following flow of traffic. Turn left at T-junction and travel 200m past St Multose Church.

BOW HALL

Dick & Barbara Vickery
Castletownshend
West Cork
Tel: (028) 36114
dvicbowhall@eircom.net

We don't know how Barbara
Vickery does what she does,
but we're sure grateful she
does what she does.

We don't want to be accused of ageism over this, but let's be honest: Barbara Vickery has seen four score years come and go effortlessly, and we don't know just how she does what she does. All we know is: we are sure grateful. What Mrs Vickery does is to marshall this house with the command of a lieutenant, and the zip of a teenager, cooking smashing breakfasts for guests, keeping her trio of Shaker-style rooms in tip-top shape, and all the time creating a vibe about this dreamy house that is simply irresistible. It's an idyllic place, and exactly the sort of house you want to find in a charming village like Castletownshend: relaxed, relaxing, stylish in an ageless way. Ageless is just the right word, come to think of it. Mrs Vickery and her house have an ageless energy and brio that is the very soul of hospitality itself, and age or ageism simply doesn't come into it: Bow Hall has the life force.

- **OPEN:** All year, except Christmas
- **ROOMS:** Three rooms, all with private baths
- **PRICE:** €45 per person sharing, Single supplement €5

- **NOTES:**
No smoking house. No credit cards accepted. Dinner 8pm, €30, communal table.
No wheelchair access.
Enclosed car park.
Children welcome, high chair, cot.

- **DIRECTIONS:**
On the right hand side of the village, heading down the steep hill.

FORTVIEW HOUSE

Violet Connell
Gurtyowen
Toormore, Goleen
West Cork
Tel & Fax: (028) 35324
fortviewhousegoleen@eircom.net

Violet Connell's West Cork farmhouse B&B is one of the most cultish of destinations, thanks to sublime cooking. *icon*

No one can resist Fortview. From the harshest food writers with the sharpest critical teeth, to ordinary decent folk who simply want to find somewhere lovely to chill out and collect themselves in comfort, Fortview is the destination above all others. Mrs Connell's cooking is perhaps the principal reason for its success – the breakfasts are sublime, the dinners superb – but there is also the house's idyllic location on the Mizen peninsula to consider – a few miles north of Goleen, and there is nothing like a few days scooting around the lovely west Cork peninsulas to set you right – and also the lovely style of the house itself, decorated by Violet with idiosyncratic individuality and expertise. Put all these things together, and you have the ultimate B&B, the critic's favourite, the people's choice, the West Cork beacon of good food, good style, good cheer and really good times.

- ● **OPEN:** 1 March-1 Nov
- ● **ROOMS:** Five rooms, all en suite
- ● **PRICE:** €40 per person sharing, B&B

● **NOTES:**
Dinner by arrangement only. Self-catering house available, sleeps six.
No wheelchair access.
Enclosed car park.
Children over 6 years welcome.

● **DIRECTIONS:**
Signposted 2km from Toormore on the main Durrus road (R591). 12km from Durrus, 9km from Goleen.

GARNISH HOUSE

Con & Hansi Lucey
Western Road
Cork City, County Cork
Tel: (021) 427 5111 Fax: 427 3872
garnish@iol.ie
www.garnish.ie

Garnish is the proud beacon of hospitality on the endless Western Road of B&B's, thanks to Hansi Lucey and her great Cork humour.

Garnish is an unremarkable house if you look at things in strict terms – no pool, small rooms, no glitzy shower, none of the starred sort of comfort that we are all supposed to want and demand everywhere we go.

But Garnish, truth be told, has all it needs, and all it needs is Hansi Lucey and her voluble, capable, maternal hospitality. There is a gentleness, a kindness, a sweetness about the Cork character that is unique in Ireland, and, for us, Mrs Lucey embodies that very spirit: you just can't imagine her working anywhere other than Cork city.

Her kindness, then, is the very animus of this house, and it is, after you have been here about two minutes, the only thing that you will notice. The endless solicitude at breakfast time, as Hansi fusses over you to make sure you have absolutely everything you could need or want, is awesome, and you set out with a spring in your step.

- **OPEN:** All year
- **ROOMS:** 14 rooms, all en suite
- **PRICE:** €40-€65 per person B&B

- **NOTES:**
No dinner. Limited wheelchair access.
Enclosed car parking.
Children welcome, high chair, cot, babysitting, reduction if sharing.
Self-catering suites available.

- **DIRECTIONS:**
Five minutes' walk from the city centre, just opposite UCC.

GLENALLY HOUSE

Fred & Herta Rigney
Copperally, Youghal
East Cork
Tel: (024) 91623
enquiries@glenally.com
www.glenally.com

Glenally proves that
aesthetics is the rescue
remedy: this is a gorgeous,
style lover's dream of a house.

Introduce Fred and Herta Rigney to a friend and your friend will whisper afterwards: 'What a striking couple!'. Indeed they are, and that individuality, that out-of-the-box characteristic, defines their gorgeous house, Glenally, just outside Youghal. This is a design lover's dream house, but above all, it is a house that is striking because of its individuality. At a time when so many modern houses all share the same sources – O'Hagan design; Foko, you name it – the Rigneys have worked from another template altogether, and the result is a modern house that is wholly individual, wholly distinct: it's a peach.

We might call the style bricolage, a collection of treasured pieces united by form and function, but where the Rigneys score is with their use of colour, and with Fred's excellent cooking. Glenally is a balm for the aesthete's soul, proof that aesthetics is a rescue remedy.

● **OPEN:** 1 Mar-mid Dec. Reservations only Dec-Feb
● **ROOMS:** Four rooms, 3 all en suite, 1 private bath
● **PRICE:** €45-€55 per person sharing,
€15 single supplement.

● **NOTES:**
Visa, Mastercard. Dinner, 8pm, €35. No wheelchair access. Secure car parking. No facilities for under 12s.

● **DIRECTIONS:**
From Youghal: From Clockgate take N25 east to roundabout. Continue straight on N25 past Esso station for 250m, and take first left. After 75m turn right and go to end of lane (200m) and through gates.

GROVE HOUSE

Billy & Mary O'Shea
Colla Road, Schull
West Cork
Tel: (028) 28067, Fax: 28069
billyoshea@yahoo.com
www.grovehouseschull.com

A great destination in funky Schull, the colourful and calm Grove House offers great hospitality and the great local foods of the west Cork artisans.

Billy and Mary O'Shea's pretty house sits high and handsome on the Colla Road, with fantastic views out across the bay at Schull. The house has become an integral part of the attraction of this pretty village, and the O'Sheas capitalise on this sense of locality with imaginative breakfast menus that make a real feature of the foods of local artisans. So, expect not just Fingal Ferguson's superb Gubbeen bacon at breakfast time, but also bespoke bangers made especially for Grove House by Fingal. Clonakilty pudding and yogurts feature, and Sally Barne's benchmark smoked salmon and smoked tuna. The eggs, meantime, are the work of happy local hens, and a fried Schull egg with some of Mary's brown bread or warm scones will put a spring in your step for the rest of the day. This is just the way to run a lovely B&B, a little local treasure and a local treasure chest.

- **OPEN:** Mar-Oct
- **ROOMS:** Five double rooms
- **PRICE:** €45-€60 high per person sharing.
Single supplement €15

- **NOTES:**
No restaurant (plenty locally). No wheelchair access. Private parking. Not suitable for children under 12.

- **DIRECTIONS:**
From Cork/Killarney take the N71 to Ballydehob, then the R592 to Schull. Proceed through village to the library. Take left turn onto Colla Road, Grove House is about 500 metres on the right-hand side.

10 PLACES WITH
GREAT STYLE

BUGGY'S GLENCAIRN INN
LISMORE, Co WATERFORD

THE CLARENCE
DUBLIN, Co DUBLIN

GLENALLY HOUSE
YOUGHAL, Co CORK

ISKEROON
BUNAVALLA, Co KERRY

THE MORRISON
DUBLIN, Co DUBLIN

THE QUAY HOUSE
CLIFDEN, Co GALWAY

RATHCOURSEY HOUSE
MIDLETON, Co CORK

SALVILLE HOUSE
ENNISCORTHY, Co WEXFORD

SHELBURNE LODGE
KENMARE, Co KERRY

TODDIES
KINSALE, Co CORK

LONGUEVILLE HOUSE

The O'Callaghan family
Mallow
North Cork
Tel: (022) 47156, Fax: 47459
info@longuevillehouse.ie
www.longuevillehouse.ie

The O'Callaghan family
have a genius for making
memories of staying at
Longueville indelible.

First time we ever ate in Longueville, we enjoyed an informal lunch in the conservatory, and it was one of those meals that you can never, ever, forget.

Well, the good news is that the beautiful Victorian conservatory – built in 1862 – has been restored to its pristine glory, and adds another aesthetic coup de grace to this magnificent house, an address distinguished by the bounteous hospitality of the O'Callaghan family. 'The Sunday in Longueville will live with me for a long time...', a friend wrote recently, and this is the gift the O'Callaghan's have: like a tiny handful of other places to stay in Ireland, Longueville creates memories, pleasures, tastes and experiences which live with you forever. It is one of the truly great places, an address where everything – but everything – is done to benchmark standard, and where standards never slip from an artful perfection.

- **OPEN:** Mar-Nov
- **ROOMS:** 20 rooms, all en suite
- **PRICE:** €170-340 B&B per room

- **NOTES:**
Dinner served from 6.30pm, €50. Recommended for vegetarians and people with special diets. No wheelchair access. Children welcome, babysitting on request, toy chest, working farm.

- **DIRECTIONS:**
3 miles west of Mallow on the N72 to Killarney. Take Ballyclough Junction to the right, and hotel entrance is 100 yards on the left hand side.

OTTO'S CREATIVE CATERING

Otto & Hilda Kunze
Dunworley, Butlerstown
Bandon, West Cork
Tel: (023) 40461
ottokunze@eircom.net
www.ottoscreativecatering.com

Spend a few days at OCC, and you may decide never to return to the 'civilised' world. Otto and Hilda's alternative way is radically profound.

Otto and Hilda Kunze simply do things differently, and in doing them differently, they do things better. Their methods of working with food, and of creating a place to stay, focus on the essentials, on the demands of our psyche: what sort of food will truly satisfy us? What sort of remote destination will truly allow us to escape from the clamour of the so-called civilised world?

Having ascertained what it is that we truly want – the purest, most elemental food imaginable, the most gorgeous location with calm, handsome and comfortable rooms and a traditional pair of cottages – then they set about creating this magic escape, this restaurant with the purest food one can eat. In creating OCC, what they have made is a spa, but not just a spa for the body: it is a spa for the soul. Of course, the extraordinary food feeds your body, but, above all, what OCC feeds is your soul.

● **OPEN:** All year
● **ROOMS:** two double rooms and self-catering cottage
● **PRICE:** €50 per person sharing, €20 single supplement.

● **NOTES:**
Visa, Mastercard. Dinner served Wed-Sun, €45.
No wheelchair access.
Secure parking.
Children welcome.

● **DIRECTIONS:**
From Bandon go to Timoleague, follow signs to Barryroe until you come across signs to Dunworley.

RATHCOURSEY HOUSE

Beth Hallinan
Ballinacurra, Midleton
East Cork
Tel: (021) 461 3418
beth@rathcoursey.com
www.rathcoursey.com

The gorgeous Rathcoursey
has become one of the
cult addresses in Ireland
in double-quick time.

It has become commonplace, already, for people to talk
about Beth Hallinan's utterly gorgeous house as THE
place where they want to head to in order to celebrate
a special event: that significant birthday or anniversary,
that healing getaway, that dreaded family reunion, that
meeting-up with beloved friends. What is significant is
that everyone loves Rathcoursey, loves the privacy of this
private house that happily takes guests, for Rathcoursey
works its magic on everyone: resistance is futile.

What's to love? Everything. The house is a gem in design
terms, one of the boldest mixes of colour, furniture and
style you will find anywhere, all of it creating an oasis that
is Rathcoursey and nowhere else. Beth's excellent
breakfasts, which show the wit and chutzpah of a
professional cook. Above all, it is the ability of the house
to summon your fantasies, to romance your own dreams.

- **OPEN:** All year
- **ROOMS:** Five double en suite rooms, one single
- **PRICE:** €95 per person sharing. Single suppl.€10

- **NOTES:**
Mastercard and Visa accepted. Dinner by special
arrangement. Full wheelchair access, plus a small sitting
room adjacent to room which could be for a carer. Car
parking in grounds. Children welcome.

- **DIRECTIONS:**
At Midleton roundabout take Whitegate exit. After 1.5
miles turn right at cross roads for East Ferry. Go
through Rathcoursey and follow mysterious arrows.

ROCK COTTAGE

Barbara Klotzer
Barnatonicane, Schull
West Cork
Tel & Fax: (028) 35538
rockcottage@eircom.net
www.mizen.net/rockcottage

Barbara Klotzer's elegant Georgian house is a fantastic West Cork getaway, a great house with a glorious menagerie of farm animals to befriend.

Rock Cottage looks as if it has dropped out of the sky onto the Mizen peninsula. How else, you wonder, could a fine Georgian house have wound up here, a few miles either side of Schull and Goleen? And, then, there is the fact that it isn't a cottage, but a proper, medium-sized Georgian house, fronted in black slate, which makes it look very glamorous and dramatic, surprising.

Barbara Klotzer works hard at every aspect of Rock Cottage, rearing a splendid menagerie of farm animals, maintaining a meticulous house, and putting serious effort into both breakfast and dinner, with tireless sourcing of the best ingredients; don't miss that Caherbeg bacon at breakfast time. This is a great chill-out zone, which feels wonderfully remote and away-from-it-all, especially the pretty self-catering cottage, a fantastic West Cork idyll. Sitting in the garden, amidst the menagerie, is some bliss.

- ● **OPEN:** All year
- ● **ROOMS:** Three rooms and self-catering cottage
- ● **PRICE:** €76-€90 per person sharing, €53-€60 single, B&B

● **NOTES:**
Visa, Mastercard. Dinner, 7.30pm, book 24hrs ahead, €32.
Children welcome, cot, working farm.

● **DIRECTIONS:**
From Schull, go west towards Goleen. At Toormore turn right onto the R591 towards Durrus. After 1.5 miles you will see their sign on the left.

SEA VIEW HOUSE HOTEL

Kathleen O'Sullivan
Ballylickey, Bantry
West Cork
Tel: (027) 50462, Fax: 51555
info@seaviewhousehotel.com
www.seaviewhousehotel.com

Sea View is the archetypal West Cork, owner-run, intimate country hotel, and then some. Nobody works harder than this team to make you happy.

Kathleen O'Sullivan knows that God is in the detail, and that scriptural urgency is the animus behind the lovely Sea View House. Everything that one might expect of a small, intimate, country hotel is raised to a sparkling high, thanks to the driven work of Ms O'Sullivan and her team. They work hard, harder than anyone else.

Sea View is one of those rare addresses which taps into our subconscious, because we all have an imagined, nostalgic concept of just what an owner-run West Cork country hotel should be like. We want it warm and welcoming, decorated in the classic style – not modern and minimalist, no way – with nice country cooking. But Ms O'Sullivan trumps our subconscious: Sea View is warmer, more welcoming, more intimate than we dared to hope. The attention to every detail in every respect gladdens the heart, and creates the hotel of our dreams.

- **OPEN:** mid Mar-mid Nov
- **ROOMS:** 25 rooms
- **PRICE:** €120-€175 per room

- **NOTES:**
All major cards accepted.
Dinner in restaurant 7pm-9pm, Sun lunch (from Easter Sun) and lounge food daily.
Dinner €40.
Full wheelchair access. Secure parking.

- **DIRECTIONS:**
On the N71 from Cork, 3 miles from Bantry and 8 miles from Glengarriff.

TODDIES

Pearse & Mary O'Sullivan
Sleaveen House, Eastern Road
Kinsale, West Cork
Tel: (021) 477 7769
toddies@eircom.net
www.toddieskinsale.com

Pearse and Mary O'Sullivan have good taste, which shines through in their three stylish suites, and their excellent, creative Kinsale restaurant.

The O'Sullivans have good taste. You might see this originally in the collection of modern Irish art which the couple have assembled and which adorns the lovely dining room of their lovely restaurant. But this good taste and good judgement extends over into the three suites which they offer to guests, which have tip-top specifications in terms of luxury, but which impress most as being calmly considered and ordered spaces that are terrifically relaxing: the feng shui is good here, just as you expected it would be.

And their restaurant is one of the few reliable, creative places to be found in a pretty town which is now living on past glories: gourmet capital? Don't think so, though Mr O'Sullivan's super cooking will go a long way to reasserting Kinsale's grasp on that title. Being just out of the town, Toddies lets you escape the Kinsale wildness.

● **OPEN:** Mar-Dec
● **ROOMS:** Three suites
● **PRICE:** €72.50 per person sharing.
Single supplement €26.50

● **NOTES:**
Visa, Mastercard, Amex.
No wheelchair access.
ISDN line.

● **DIRECTIONS:**
On entering Kinsale from the Cork side pass Texaco Station (right hand side). They are the 4th house on the left, painted yellow.

CASTLE MURRAY HOUSE HOTEL

Marguerite Howley
Dunkineely
County Donegal
Tel: (073) 37022
castlemurray@eircom.net
www.castlemurray.com

Marguerite Howley has taken over the reins at Castle Murray, the pioneering Donegal restaurant with rooms where she learnt her trade: so far, so good.

Marguerite Howley has moved from the highly regarded Fleet Inn in Killybegs (now run by the Bach family), and travelled a few miles down the coast to her old stomping ground of Castle Murray House, the place where she learnt her craft with Thierry Delcros. The transition has been smooth: Remy Dupas remains in the kitchen, Sunday lunch is still a big day out for the locals, and the emphasis of the restaurant remains focused on seafood, whilst the accommodation is still simple and extremely good value. All in all, what Castle Murray offers is an expert package, a chance to get away to the wilds of Donegal and have lovely food, stay in a relaxing room, enjoy some of the most unbelievably beautiful views in Ireland, and chill out, big time, without breaking the bank. The cooking shows an honest culinary freehand, the staff are truly welcoming, and Castle Murray is set fair for success.

- **OPEN:** All year
- **ROOMS:** Ten rooms
- **PRICE:** €48 per person sharing.
Single supplement €71

- **NOTES:**
Visa, Mastercard.
No wheelchair access.
Children welcome.

- **DIRECTIONS:**
Dunkineely is west of Donegal town, and Castle Murray is signposted just west of the village, on the N56 road from Donegal to Killybegs.

COXTOWN MANOR

Edward Dewael
Laghey
County Donegal
Tel: (073) 34574, Fax: 34576
coxtownmanor@oceanfree.net
www.coxtownmanor.com

A Belgian-Irish fusion of tastes and talents proves to be a winner at Edward Dewael's fine, hospitable, country house and restaurant.

Coxtown is a winner, thanks to Ed Dewael's excellent, principled and tasty cooking, and helpful staff whose unpretentious local manner is disarmingly charming. It's a big house, but thriftily renovated, and focused on comfort rather than grandness. There is an air of relaxed control about the place which is simply infectious: you could almost imagine you are visiting friends for a night's stay and a chatty dinner. But, if your friends could cook as well as Mr Dewael, you would be a happy camper; this is thoughtful, controlled cooking, which is very strong on meticulous sourcing of the foods; local beef and lamb; fresh seafood, and with memorable desserts to bring things to a rousing climax. Don't miss the seafood, despite the allure of the meat cookery, and don't miss the excellent Belgian beers. Friendly, charming Coxtown is just the ticket, a cute little escape dedicated to simplicity.

- **OPEN:** All year, except early spring
- **ROOMS:** Five rooms
- **PRICE:** €55 per person sharing. Single supplement €19

- **NOTES:**
Visa, Mastercard, Laser.
Dinner, 7pm-9pm.
Rates for Dinner & B&B available.
Children welcome - family rooms

- **DIRECTIONS:**
Look for their sign on the N15 between Ballyshannon and Donegal, turning just before the Esso station.

CROAGHROSS

John & Kay Deane
Portsalon, Letterkenny
County Donegal
Tel: (074) 59548, Fax: 59546
jkdeane@croaghross.com
www.croaghross.com

The Deanes are a great double act, swopping and switching tasks with great vigour and gifting the lovely Croaghross with great energy.

Perhaps it is because John and Kay Deane are such a capable, efficient double-act, alternating the tasks of meeting and greeting, and cooking and serving in Croaghross with such ease, that this explains why this pretty house has such energy. Then again, with the wild Donegal air whipping up the hill from the stupendous Portsalon strand, who wouldn't be fired-up with energy: that fresh air is inspiring, and it puts a spring in your step. Mind you, people who are at Croaghross for the first time can find the sheer elementalism of the place almost disabling: you can see them almost nodding off as the evening comes to a close, worn out with all that natural goodness. Mind you, they are also likely sated by some excellent cooking – don't miss the cod with crème fraîche and cherry tomatoes! – and some lovely wines, the perfect conclusion to a perfect day in Croaghross.

- **OPEN:** Mar-Oct (off season by arrangement)
- **ROOMS:** Five double rooms, three en suite, two with showers.
- **PRICE:** €35-50 per person sharing, Single suppl. €6.50

- **NOTES:**
All major cards. Dinner, €27.50. Children welcome, high tea by arrangement. Cottage available for families. Recommended for vegetarians. Full wheelchair access.

- **DIRECTIONS:**
In Portsalon, turn right at crossroads, continue past church and golf course, take small road on left, house half mile on left.

THE GREEN GATE

Paul Chatenoud
Ardvally
Ardara
County Donegal
Tel: (075) 41546

The Green Gate is one of the most
unlikely cult addresses in the country.
If you seek solace from mod cons,
then it's for you: get it in your soul.

Against all the odds, Paul Chatenoud's little cottage and
its collection of outhouses has become a cult address.

So, what were the odds? Well, this is a very Spartan place
to stay; very simple, very elemental, but lacking any sort
of mod cons or luxury doodahs which many people
expect when they are touring on holiday.

But, maybe M. Chatenoud knows better. Maybe he knows
that what people want is not trouser presses and power
showers, but someplace in which they can take a deep
breath, allow themselves to be overpowered by the
natural beauty of the landscape, and retreat into
themselves, into their soul. Maybe M. Chatenoud knows
that a real spa offers only the simplicity of your own
introspection. Whatever, he finds himself a cult figure with
a cult address. Magic, mystical, wild, TGG also offers the
largest selection of breakfast conserves in Ireland.

- ● **OPEN:** All year
- ● **ROOMS:** Four rooms, all en suite
- ● **PRICE:** €30-40 per person

● **NOTES:**
No dinner.
No credit cards.
Wheelchair access.
Private parking.
Children welcome.

● **DIRECTIONS:**
A mile east of Ardara, way, way up the hill, and
signposted from the road.

THE MILL

Derek and Susan Alcorn
Figart, Dunfanaghy
County Donegal
Tel & Fax: (074) 36985
info@themillrestaurant.com
www.themillrestaurant.com

A pretty house in a sublime location, with great cooking and superb value for money is The Mill's smart recipe for success in this great address.

Splendid cooking and a serene professionalism have ensured the success of The Mill right from when Susan and Derek Alcon opened their doors. The mix is congratulated by the splendidly designed rooms – the artist Frank Eggington, whose house and studio this was, would have been delighted with such restraint and such a sure eye for detail – and by the fabulous natural beauty of the area: if you can secure a room with views out across New Lake, then go for it: the sunsets are sublime. But another key to their success has been the value for money in both dinner and accommodation which have been bringing back punters from day one. This ability to balance everything, and to make it all work with such seeming ease, explains the sure-footed style of this excellent address. Go once, and you will back again to let a little more of that Donegal magic into your life.

● **OPEN:** Easter-Hallowe'en, open every night
● **ROOMS:** Six rooms
● **PRICE:** €38 per person sharing.
Single supplement €7

● **NOTES:**
Visa, Mastercard, Amex. Restaurant open Tue-Sun, dinner, €33. No wheelchair access.
Children welcome - children's menu, travel cot, babysitting if needed.

● **DIRECTIONS:**
Take N56 through Dunfanaghy. The Mill is situated a half mile past the village, on the right, beside the lake.

ROSSAOR HOUSE

Brian & Anne Harkin
Ballyliffin, Inishowen
County Donegal
Tel & Fax: (077) 76498
rossaor@gofree.indigo.ie
www.ballyliffin.com/rossaor.htm

Rossaor is a benchmark B&B, a place where guests discover the peace that comes with great hospitality and the fine cooking of our friends up North.

Inishowen is a magnet for landscape painters, guys and girls with easels and palettes and a determination to finally capture the wildly elusive patterns of light that bless this beautiful part of the country. But, even if you lack the easel and the palette, you owe it to yourself to have a few days in the company of this mesmerising – and we don't use that word lightly – landscape, and your destination, then, should be Rossaor.

This is a B&B as B&B's should be: hearty hosts, comfortable rooms and public rooms, fantastic breakfasts. To be perfectly honest, Rossaor is so comfortable that it takes a fair act of will, after a lazy, lingering breakfast, to actually get yourself up and running and out of the doors into that mesmerising landscape. Brian and Anne look after everyone so well that virtually everyone who stays here is a regular visitor, a convert.

- **OPEN:** All year, except Christmas and New Year
- **ROOMS:** 4 rooms, all en suite, (incl 3 family rooms)
- **PRICE:** €35 per person sharing. Single supplement €10

- **NOTES:**
Mastercard, Visa. No dinner. Partial wheelchair access (a couple of steps at main entrance). Private car parking. Children accepted, but no facilities.

- **DIRECTIONS:**
Go to Buncrana, follow the R238 to Clonmany, Ballyliffin is 1.5 miles further on, still on the R238. House is about 100 yards past the Strand Hotel, on the left going towards the golf club.

10 PLACES NEAR MAJOR
ROADS, PORTS & AIRPORTS

ABERDEEN LODGE
DUBLIN PORTS

AN BOHREEN
THE N25

BALLYTEIGUE
SHANNON AIRPORT

CHURCHTOWN
ROSSLARE PORT

LEGENDS GUESTHOUSE
THE N8

THE MOAT INN
BELFAST INTERNATIONAL AIRPORT

THE MUSTARD SEED
SHANNON AIRPORT

PRESTON HOUSE
THE N7

THE RED BANK
DUBLIN PORT & AIRPORT

WINEPORT LODGE
THE N4

ABERDEEN LODGE

Pat Halpin
53-55 Park Avenue
Ballsbridge, Dublin 4
Tel: (01) 283 8155, Fax: 283 7877
aberdeen@iol.ie
www.halpinsprivatehotels.com

Regular guests love the care lavished on them in Aberdeen, a townhouse that lets you feel far away from the city rush and gives space to relax.

'It is an extremely relaxing, quiet, comfortable place, and I would go back.'

They sure know how to knock out a good summary, do our Bridgestone editors, and you really can't say anything more defining about Pat Halpin's spruce Ballsbridge address than that concise report. Good coffee and homemade biscuits are just the ticket when you arrive, and the calm colours and smart housekeeping are very reassuring. Breakfasts are excellent: a fine buffet of fruits, breads, cereals and juices, and good cooked breakfasts which show real care. It's easy to see why Aberdeen has devoted regulars, people who want the attention and care of a house where you are both looked after, and yet left alone with time to think, where you are given just the right sort of space by the staff. Terrific location, of course, and proximity to the DART means you can forget the car.

● **OPEN:** All year
● **ROOMS:** 17 rooms, including two suites
● **PRICE:** €65-€90 per person sharing, €99-€120 single

● **NOTES:**
Light 'drawing room' menu, €8-€15 per course, extensive wine list. Secure parking.
Wheelchair access.
Children - not suitable for children under 7yrs.

● **DIRECTIONS:**
Just down from the Sydney Parade DART station. Park Avenue runs parallel with Merrion Road & Strand Road.

BROWNE'S

Barry J Canny
22 St Stephen's Green, Dublin 2
Tel: (01) 638 3939
Fax: (01) 638 3900
brownesdublin@eircom.net
www.brownesdublin.com

Location! Location! Location! Browne's fab situation on St Stephen's Green puts you at the heart of the city, and you avoid gridlock.

There are other addresses on St Stephen's Green, but Browne's is unquestionably the one to choose over other – much pricier – hotels and townhouses. Staying in this intimate house, characterised by very efficient and personable staff, you do feel that you are right at the centre of the city, which is hardly surprising: you are.

Preserving and protecting the character of the building was owner Barry Canny's toughest challenge, but his hard work has paid off, and how nice to stay in a true Georgian townhouse – Browne's dates from 1790, when it was constructed by Sir Thomas Leighton – which has been restored with so much care. But Browne's is also notable for staff who are attentive and welcoming, which sadly is not something that can be taken for granted in Dublin these days. It's a little treasure at the heart of the city, a clubbable, comfortable destination. You'll be back.

● **OPEN:** All year, except 24 Dec-3 Jan
● **ROOMS:** 11 rooms: deluxe, superior, suite, single, twin
● **PRICE:** B&B - Single €185, Double €225, Deluxe €255

● **NOTES:**
Restaurant open 7am-10.30am, 12.30pm-3pm lunch and 6.30pm-11pm dinner all week (no lunch Sat). No wheelchair access. Street parking. Locked car parks nearby on the Green. No facilities for children.

● **DIRECTIONS:**
30 mins driving from Dublin airport, 5 mins from Trinity College, 1 min from Grafton Street.

THE CLARENCE

Robert van Eerde
6-8 Wellington Quay
Dublin 2
Tel: (01) 407 0800, Fax: 407 0820
reservations@theclarence.ie
www.theclarence.ie

Expensive, and worth it, the Clarence hotel proves that classic design is ageless, and agelessly pleasing.

icon

It costs a lot to stay in The Clarence, and it's worth it. Other city addresses have tried to emulate the baroque style of this great hotel, but the original remains the best: this is a feel-good zone, a place where everything works to make you feel fabulous, from the glorious aesthetic of the design with its understatement, to the fabulous food produced by Antony Ely and his team.

Mr Ely has made the reputation of The Tea Room for his cooking at lunch and dinner, but breakfast here shares his precise, light and very focused approach to cooking. The Tea Room breakfast is the best in the city – if you want to do a breakfast meeting with Estragon Press, then please bring us here! – and the staff who serve it are charming. Time and again, as we look back on our notes after staying here, everything concludes with 'this is the best hotel, our favourite hotel'. Indeed it is: a true classic.

- **OPEN:** All year
- **ROOMS:** 49 rooms, incl penthouse & suites
- **PRICE:** €300-640 per person sharing

- **NOTES:**
All major credit cards accepted. Full wheelchair access. Valet parking.
Children welcome, cots, toys, video games, children's meals.

- **DIRECTIONS:**
Overlooking the River Liffey, on the South side, approximately 150 metres up from the Ha'penny Bridge. 30-45 minutes' drive from Dublin airport.

THE HIBERNIAN HOTEL

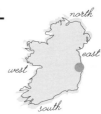

Barry Wyse/PJ Daly
Eastmoreland Place
Ballsbridge, Dublin 4
Tel: (01) 668 7666, Fax: 660 2655
info@hibernianhotel.ie
www.hibernianhotel.com

Thank heavens for the Hib, a hospitable antidote to the like-it-or-lump-it attitude prevalent in Dublin hotels.

The casual indifference of staff in so many Dublin hotels these days is a matter for not merely regret, but actual concern. When a waiter takes back a breakfast plate which has hardly been touched, and makes no effort to enquire what was wrong, then things have reached a sad stage of decline. That very thing happened to us when researching for this book: a €19 plate of rubbish served in a €200-a-night hotel. Dear, oh dear.

So, all praise to the friendly, personable Hibernian, one of those hotels where – remember this? – the staff actually look after you. They care about your welfare, your satisfaction. They remember your name. They care that breakfast is a good meal, that dinner is a treat, that at all times you should have what you want, what you need. The staff here are a tribute to true Dublin hospitality, and they make the Hib a key city address, an hospitable address.

- **OPEN:** All year, except Christmas
- **ROOMS:** 40 rooms, all en suite
- **PRICE:** €222-€237 per room. €277.50 junior suite

- **NOTES:**
Dinner 6.30pm-10pm (7pm-9pm Sun, residents only)
Full wheelchair access.
Off-street parking.
Children welcome, high chair, cot.

- **DIRECTIONS:**
Where Upper Baggot Street meets Pembroke Road. The Hibernian directly faces St Mary's Road. On the same side of the street as the AIB bank.

MARBLE HALL

Shelagh Conway
81 Marlborough Road
Donnybrook, Dublin 4
Tel: (01) 497 7350
marblehall@eircom.net
www.marblehall.ie

Shelagh Conway's smart D4
Georgian house is one of the
very best city B&B's, and
with one of the best breakfasts.

Dublin has become a city in which getting a good breakfast has become almost impossible, so thank the stars for Marble Hall. Shelagh Conway's breakfast is precise, perfect, delicious, everything a cooked Irish breakfast should be: there are beautifully poached fruits, creamy yogurts, superb breads and hot toast, and a cooked breakfast worthy of an award: sweet bacon; excellent Clonakilty puddings, fresh eggs, peppery sausages, all beautifully cooked, served with hot tea. This is as good as it gets.

But then, making sure that everything is as good as it gets is Ms Conway's métier. The house is calmly and correctly decorated, the rooms are comfy, the beds high and handsome, and the overall feeling is one of great comfort, abetted by great hospitality: this is a major new address, so flee those hotels and get up to Donnybrook.

- **OPEN:** All year
- **ROOMS:** Three rooms
- **PRICE:** €50 per person sharing, Single €75

- **NOTES:**
Visa, Mastercard. Not suitable for children.
No wheelchair access. No dinner.
Secure parking.

- **DIRECTIONS:**
Marlborough Road runs between Ranelagh and Donnybrook villages. Marble Hall is on the right hand side, near the top of the road, driving from Donnybrook to Ranelagh.

THE MORRISON

Anthony Kenna
Ormond Quay
Dublin 1
Tel: (01) 887 2400, Fax: 874 4039
info@morrisonhotel.ie
www.morrisonhotel.ie

The Morrison has the most interesting use of colour in any city hotel, creating an earthy tactility.

We like the attention to tactile detail that you find in The Morrison, the weave of the throw on the bed with its ivory tones set against the sheer white, the cinnamon sticks in the glass bowl on the table, the granite sink, the tactility of the dark wood used throughout, and the views from the front rooms, out across the Millennium Bridge and the River Liffey, are simply to die for. The hotel itself has settled down from the intense self-consciousness which characterised it in the early days; indeed, Jean-Michel Poulot and his team in the Halo restaurant are cooking some of the very finest food in Dublin, and the room is superbly managed. To be honest, The Morrison is a real feel-good place, and its secret is that it is never banal, it won't allow itself to be commonplace, and the team here work hard to keep it right up to scratch. It's a great city address, for sure.

- **OPEN:** All year, except 25-26 Dec
- **ROOMS:** 90 rooms and suites, incl penthouse
- **PRICE:** From €270 per room

- **NOTES:**
All major cards accepted. Wheelchair access. Children welcome. Street parking and rate offered in Jervis St Car Park.
Halo Restaurant and Cafe Bar open daily. Lobo, late night club open till 3am.

- **DIRECTIONS:**
Overlooking the north side of the River Liffey, just opposite the new Millennium Bridge on Ormond Quay.

NUMBER 31

Noel & Deirdre Comer
31 Leeson Close
Dublin 2
Tel: (01) 676 5011, Fax: 676 2929
number31@iol.ie
www.number31.ie

Do you want to be James
Bond, or James Joyce?
Number 31 lets you choose
which Jemmy you want to be.

Like the very best hosts, Noel Comer is not just a good
guide to his house, but a good guide to his city. It's typical
of the care of the Comers that they should always ensure
that they are so well briefed about what is going on in the
big smoke, a vital attribute that so many others in the
hospitality business overlook, or simply don't bother to
familiarise themselves with.

If Mr Comer is good on the macro picture, he is equally
good at the micro picture, setting you at your ease as you
settle into this cult address, one of the most favoured
houses in the Bridgestone guides. The house comprises
an ultra-modern mews, and a traditional Georgian house,
so whether you want to travel back to the style of the
1960's or the style of the 1860's is up to you. But, the
location is perfect, breakfasts are great, and there are
always fascinating people staying here, as hip as yourself.

● **OPEN:** All year
● **ROOMS:** 21 rooms, all en suite
● **PRICE:** €175-€199 double room rate. Single
occupancy €140

● **NOTES:**
Visa, Mastercard, Amex. Wheelchair access with
assistance. Locked parking. Children over 10 years
welcome, but no facilities.

● **DIRECTIONS:**
From St Stephen's Green. Turn right at 3rd set of traffic
lights onto Pembroke St, left at end, to Leeson St lower.
Look for Cooper's - the Close is on a laneway beside it.

THE RED BANK LODGE

Terry McCoy
5-7 Church Street, Skerries
County Dublin
Tel: (01) 849 1005, Fax: 849 1598
redbank@eircom.net
www.redbank.ie

Terry McCoy has great developments at foot in the Red Bank House, adding new rooms to create a key new destination in pretty Skerries.

It is difficult nowadays, at a time when Skerries has been swallowed up by new housing to become a satellite of Dublin, to believe that the town was once a seaside resort all in its own right. But if the place has changed, there still remains something of the spirit of the old Skerries about the town, and for someone who plans a trip to eat Terry McCoy's excellent seafood cookery in The Red Bank, then the new developments with this dynamic venture, which will see it having 18 rooms by the middle of the year, will turn the trip northside into an event, a chance to grab some quality time away from the maddening city in a great escape destination, at great value. Mr McCoy is a fine cook, and his restaurant is a model of professionalism, all the better for having no truck with modernist design, and continuing to do things in the timeless, hospitable way. So, get some quality time!

- **OPEN:** All year
- **ROOMS:** 18 rooms, all en suite
- **PRICE:** From €45 per person sharing

- **NOTES:**
All major cards accepted. Restaurant open for dinner and Sunday lunch. On street parking.
Children under 5 free. Wheelchair access. Special offer, €90 dinner B&B.

- **DIRECTIONS:**
Skerries is 29km north of the centre of Dublin, and 20 minutes' drive north from Dublin airport. The guesthouse is on the sea front.

BALLYNAHINCH CASTLE

Patrick O'Flaherty
Ballinafad, Recess, Connemara
County Galway
Tel & Fax: (095) 31006
bhinch@iol.ie
www.ballynahinch-castle.com

> Ballynahinch is a sure bet,
> an otherwordly destination
> that manages to delight
> absolutely everyone.

Ballynahinch is a place that can ring our Pavlovian bells until we are all ding-dong dizzy with delight. Every detail seeks to satisfy our subconscious: the turn off the main road down into a secret place; the scale of the castle with its grandeur but lack of pretension; the blazing fire as you step into the lobby; the row of fishing lines under the stairs; the democratic charm of the bar; the romance of the dining room with its sublime views; the affable engagement of the staff; the serene air of relaxation that can only come from a whole bunch of people being, like, totally chilled out. It is a brilliant mix of hospitality, style, and a very western wit, and there is no one who can remain immune to its charms. Ballynahinch is a star.
Manager Patrick O'Flaherty runs this big pile with great ability, and chef Robert Webster's fine cooking turns a stay at Ballynahinch into a sure bet. A great destination.

● **OPEN:** 1 Mar-31 Jan
● **ROOMS:** 40 rooms, including three suites
● **PRICE:** €81-€197 per person sharing, single supplement €27

● **NOTES:**
All major cards accepted. Dinner in restaurant, €42. Full wheelchair access. Children welcome.

● **DIRECTIONS:**
As you approach Galway, follow the signs for the city. As you get closer, look out for signs for Clifden (N59). Pass through Oughterard, Moycullen, then Maam Cross, then Recess, and you will begin to see their signs.

DELPHI LODGE

Peter Mantle
Leenane
County Galway
Tel: (095) 42222, Fax: (095) 42296
delfish@iol.ie
www.delphilodge.ie

You reckon beautiful Delphi is just a place for the boys to bring their toys? Think again: this is a house women love, thanks to its soulful luxury.

Delphi has a bit of a macho mystique about it, it is the sort of place that gives an impression of Boys with their Toys: huntin', shootin', fishin', billiards, claret and chops. Funny, then, that it is actually our female Bridgestone editors who tend to rave most about Peter Mantle's fine, celebrated house, and these are not girls likely to clamber into a sou'wester and a big pair of waders just because someone thinks they might have smelt a fish. Let's be honest: these girls want to curl up on a couch with a good book and have someone bring them some tea and fruit cake because it's already 3.30pm, and by the way, what shall we be having for dinner? That's Delphi: relaxed for the ladies, invigorating for the blokes. It is a clever mixture; the essence of the country house sporting challenge, and the relaxed, laid-back Sybaritic comfort and luxury of being miles away from everything and everyone.

- **OPEN:** Mid Jan-mid Dec
- **ROOMS:** 12 rooms, all en suite (seven with lake view)
- **PRICE:** €60 standard, €120 lake view per person sharing

- **NOTES:**
Visa & Mastercard. Dinner at 8pm, communal €45. Limited wheelchair access. Secure parking. Young children discouraged.

- **DIRECTIONS:**
8 miles northwest of Leenane on the Louisburgh road. In woods on left about half mile after the Mountain Resort & Spa.

DEVON DELL

Berna Kelly
47 Devon Park
Lower Salthill, Galway city
Tel: (091) 528306
devondell@iol.ie
www.devondell.com

A peach of a Galway B&B,
Devon Dell is a definition
of cosy and comfortable,
helpful and hospitable.

Berna Kelly is one of the great B&B keepers, her manner all care and concern, hard work, attention to detail, all of it founded in an utterly true hospitality that gladdens the heart. Hospitality this instinctive is a joy, and tied to such an acute level of discipline when it comes to preparing her house and cooking breakfasts, it makes for a combination that just can't be beat. You feel mothered, you feel taken care of and – suddenly – you don't have a care in the world. You are having the great time in Galway. The house is small, prim, pretty, decorated with good, timeless taste. The choice at breakfast is as staggering as the care and attention lavished on every manner of breakfast treat from French toast to kippers, poached plums to apple and nut waffle with maple syrup. Do note that Marble Hall, in Dublin, is run by Berna's sister, Sheelagh, and run with the same exacting hospitality.

- **OPEN:** Feb-Oct
- **ROOMS:** 2 double rooms, 1 twin, & 1 single, en suite
- **PRICE:** €38 per person sharing

- **NOTES:**
No credit cards. No meals. No smoking house. No wheelchair access. Secure parking. No facilities for children.

- **DIRECTIONS:**
Get onto the Fr Griffin Rd, at bottom of town, and follow to T-junction, where you take left into Lr Salthill rd. After approx 500 metres, having passed two pubs, take first right. Go 100 metres to fork in road, take left and very sharp left into cul-de-sac.

DOLPHIN BEACH

The Foyle family
Lower Sky Road, Clifden
Connemara, County Galway
Tel: (095) 21204, Fax: 22935
dolphinbeach@iol.free.ie
connemara.net/dolphinbeachhouse

Dolphin Beach is a house
that has the magic:
extraordinary location, fab
house, great hospitality.

Aeons ago, in Connemara, we asked an Italian gentleman what had most surprised him about Ireland. 'The light!' he replied. Well, if you want to see and study that light – its gradations, its inflections and colours, its moods and changes, its glory and its ebb and flow – then take yourself to the wonderful Dolphin Beach, sit in the breakfast conservatory looking out westwards, and prepare to be amazed: The light! The light!

Mind you, design lovers will spend all their time looking inwards, for Billy and Barbara Folye's lovely house is a real beaut, intriguingly designed, with achingly tall, romantic rooms and brilliant bathrooms. Dolphin is a real find, and its location, on the lower Sky Road, is magical: all of Connemara seems to be summed up in this mystical place. Lovely cooking from Sinead Foyle completes a truly blissful place to stay: Dolphin Beach really has the magic.

- **OPEN:** Feb-1 Dec
- **ROOMS:** Nine rooms, all en suite
- **PRICE:** €65-75 per person sharing. Single supplement €20

- **NOTES:**
Dinner 7pm, €37.
Enclosed parking. Children over 12 welcome.
Wheelchair access.

- **DIRECTIONS:**
Take the Sky road out of Clifden, take the lower fork for 1 mile. It's the house on the sea side. Clifden is approximately 1 hour's drive from Galway.

FERMOYLE LODGE

Nicola Stronach & J-P Maire
Costello, Connemara
County Galway
Tel: (091) 786111, Fax: 786154
fermoylelodge@eircom.net
www.fermoylelodge.com

Remote, romantic, mysterious, Fermoyle is a glorious house, but give it plenty of time to allow yourself to sink deep into its rarefied otherness.

A lot of people come to Fermoyle and stay for a week, and if you are going to make your way over here to this remote, elemental, windswept, romantic, achingly beautiful part of Connemara, on the winding, meandering, time-forgotten road that spears between Oughterard and Rossaveal, then you should set aside a week also. Fermoyle is all about vanishing: into the elements, into this great house, into the indulgence of time for yourself, time apart.

The house is a design jewel which Nicola Stronach has orchestrated with the eye of a woman who knows just what belongs where. The colours, the scale, the comfort all elide into a tone poem of good taste, the sort of good taste that flatters your choice in coming here. And, then, J-P Maire cooks in a professional French style to ensure dinner is a treat, and be sure not to miss the fine wines.

- **OPEN:** Apr-Oct
- **ROOMS:** six rooms, all with private bathrooms
- **PRICE:** €85 per person sharing, B&B

- **NOTES:**
Visa, Mastercard. Dinner €40, 7.30pm, 24 hours' notice required (any special diets should be mentioned when booking). No wheelchair access. Secure parking. Not suitable for young children.

- **DIRECTIONS:**
From Galway, take the N59 towards Clifden. In Oughterard, turn left before the bridge at The Bridge Restaurant. Lodge is 10 miles from Oughterard on right.

HARBOUR HOTEL

Sinead O'Reilly
New Dock Road
Galway, County Galway
Tel: (091) 569466, Fax: 569455
stay@harbour.ie
www.galwayharbourhotel.com

Good rooms and good value and a good location make the Harbour a smart Galway city choice; they need to sort out the breakfast offer, mind you.

Galway's restless development has spawned many new hotels, from budget boxes all the way up to the stylish – and very expensive – Radisson. The Harbour Hotel strikes a nice balance somewhere in between: value is very keen, the staff at check-in are superb, there is free car parking, it takes 90 seconds to walk into town, and the rooms are very good indeed; spacious, decked in neutral modern colours, with big bathrooms that only suffer from overly loud extractor fans. Little touches such as CD players are more than one expects in this price range, and show the smart thinking behind this set up.

It's a pity, then, that breakfast in the restaurant lets down the hard work of everyone else in the hotel. Sloppy food, sloppy service and a dull room are not what you need. So, be smart, and take that 90 second walk into town and have breakfast in Goya's or Delight: now you're talking.

- **OPEN:** All year
- **ROOMS:** 96 rooms, including those with harbour view, and executive rooms
- **PRICE:** €49-€79 per person sharing, €92 single., €40 to upgrade to superior room

- **NOTES:**
All major credit cards accepted. Restaurant and bar serve lunch, dinner and snacks. Complimentary secure parking. Conference facilities. Children welcome.

- **DIRECTIONS:**
Follow signs to the harbour, and the hotel is on your left hand side as you approach the city centre.

GARRAUNBAUN HOUSE

John & Catherine Finnegan
Moyard
Connemara
County Galway
Tel: (095) 41649, Fax: 41649
garraunbaun.house@ireland.com

Garraunbaun's view of the twelve Ben mountains is one of the most spectacular views in Ireland.

There are several houses in the Bridgestone guides which have views that are simply to die for – Moy House, An Carn, Fermoyle Lodge, Dolphin Beach, Castlemurray House – but the view of the 12 Bens from the garden of Garraunbaun on a fine clear summer day is one of the most extraordinary, spectacular and humbling that you will find anywhere in Ireland. You look out at the hills in the distance, and you feel you are at the centre of the universe, the focus of an extraordinary landscape.

It's typical of the sort of consideration used when this beautiful house was built in 1850 that the view should be so manifest, for here is a place where everything is deeply considered. The comfort of the house, its gracious spaces, its timeless elegance, combined with its location, add up to one of the great Connemara addresses. Delia Finnegan's cooking completes the spell of a magical place.

● **OPEN:** All year
● **ROOMS:** Four rooms, all with private bathroom
● **PRICE:** €45-70 per person

● **NOTES:**
Dinner, 8pm, €25, separate or communal tables. No wheelchair access.
Enclosed car park. Children welcome, high chair, cot, babysitting, video films for all ages.

● **DIRECTIONS:**
From Galway take the Clifden rd, from Clifden take the Westport rd, and 9 miles further the Garraunbaun sign is on left hand side.

KILMURVEY HOUSE

Treasa & Bertie Joyce
Kilmurvey Bay, Inis Mor
Aran Islands, County Galway
Tel: (099) 61218, Fax: (099) 61397
kilmurveyhouse@eircom.net
www.kilmurveyhouse.com

Put beautiful Kilmurvey Bay together
with beautiful Kilmurvey House and
you have the perfect Aran Island
recipe for the best times imaginable.

Kilmurvey Bay is one of our favourite places to go
swimming in Ireland, the sea crystal-clear, the sand
mother-of-pearl white, the graceful arc of the beach like
some undiscovered Mediterranean secret.

What a boon, then, that Treasa Joyce's lovely house
should be set so close to Kilmurvey Bay, and not much
more than a few minutes' jaunt by bus up the road from
Kilronan. If Kilmurvey Bay is the Aran Island beach of your
dreams, then Kilmurvey House is the Aran Island B&B of
your dreams. Great housekeeping – hang on, make that
superlative housekeeping – great domestic cooking with
both bumper breakfasts – not too much, you're going
swimming! – and lovely, comforting dinners for when you
get back, sun-scorched, exhausted – and you are very
quickly going to feel like that cat who got the cream.
Great hospitality means taking your leave won't be easy.

- **OPEN:** 1 Apr-16 Oct
- **ROOMS:** 12 rooms, all en suite (seven family rooms)
- **PRICE:** €35-€40 per person sharing. Single €50-€60

- **NOTES:**
Dinner €24, 7pm, please book in advance.
No wheelchair access.
Children welcome.

- **DIRECTIONS:**
Take boat from Rosaveel in Connemara. When you
arrive in Kilronan, the house is a further 7km from the
ferry port. On arrival, take one of the tour buses that
crowd down at the port.

NORMAN VILLA

Mark & Dee Keogh
86 Lower Salthill
Galway city
Tel & Fax: (091) 521131
normanvilla@oceanfree.net
www.normanvilla.com

The art collection is fabulous, but Mark and Dee Keogh are artists themselves: artists of genuine, true hospitality.

It is a tribute to their beautifully composed and considered house that, every time Mark and Dee Keogh buy another painting by a contemporary Irish artist, the art work not merely fits into their house, but looks as if that particular wall in the sitting room or dining room was the place for which it was always destined. It's an effect which Norman Villa shares with Ballymaloe House: both houses are, in essence, frames, gallery space, for their superb collections of paintings.

But, Norman may be as smart as a gallery, but the happy, pulsing heart of this house is the energised hospitality of the owners. They are restless self-improvers, always tweaking, correcting, adjusting, with everything from the furnishings to the breakfast offer. Their work is as much a part of the art as the glorious paintings to which they are devoted, and artists of true hospitality is what they are.

- **OPEN:** Mar-31 Oct
- **ROOMS:** Four double rooms, two family rooms
- **PRICE:** €50 per person sharing for room and continental breakfast.

- **NOTES:**
No dinner (plenty of local restaurants). No wheelchair access. Secure parking. No facilities for children under 12 years.

- **DIRECTIONS:**
Follow signs to Salthill, then to Lower Salthill. House is next door to PJ Flahertys pub, 15 minutes to the city centre.

THE QUAY HOUSE

Paddy & Julie Foyle
Beach Road, Clifden
Connemara, County Galway
Tel: (095) 21369, Fax: 21608
thequay@iol.ie
www.thequayhouse.com

Paddy Foyle is the guv'nor:
the master of hospitality,
the most hospitable man
on the Connemara block.

It's a marvellous thing to listen to Paddy Foyle on the telephone, chatting to a punter as he takes a booking. It takes all of about, oh... 45 seconds, before he has the punter chatting away, revealing all to his new best friend. But then, that is how Folye operates. He gives everything of himself to the business of hospitality: what you see is what you get, and you get everything from this genial big man, his time and energy, his enthusiasms and passions, his incredible abilities as cook and designer. Everything at Quay House is super-charged; none more so than the design of the house, with its magnificent tactility, its wit and knowingness, its sheer unpredictability, so make sure to always book a different room every time you stay, for each is as surprising, as remarkable, as any other. But everything about Quay House is remarkable, better than the norm, spontaneous, artistic, and totally unforgettable.

- **OPEN:** Mid Mar-Early-Nov
- **ROOMS:** 14 en suite rooms, including rooms with kitchens
- **PRICE:** €135 per room, B&B, €20 single supplement

- **NOTES:**
Visa, Mastercard. No dinner, but snacks on request, and plenty of local restaurants.
Full wheelchair access. Street parking. Children welcomed and encouraged.

- **DIRECTIONS:**
Take the N59 from Galway to Clifden. The Quay House is down on the quays, overlooking the harbour.

RADHARC AN CHLAIR

Mrs Brid Poíl
Inis Oirr
Aran Islands
County Galway
Tel: (099) 75019
Fax: (099) 75019

Brid Poíl's comfy, home-from-home bungalow is just the comfort you need when faced with the existential dramas that await you on Inis Oirr.

Inis Oirr has a strange sense of mystery about it, a sense of wonder and apartness. There is something about this island which is not easily understood, a sense of difference which is awesome. You come back to the island time and again, but can't seem to fathom it any better. It's more than a little unsettling, an existential drama.

But, lucky traveller, the comfort you need will be found in Brid Poíl's lovely bungalow B&B, and you should be in no doubt that this will be the perfect shelter from your existential storm. She is a fastidious lady, Mrs Poíl, a mainlander from County Clare, and she is justifiably proud of her house, of her hospitality, and of her cooking. She is a fine cook, a fine baker, and even the simplest cup of tea with a home-baked scone is a treat, whilst dinner is a feast of home cooking sharpened by the skill of someone who loves the art and craft of the kitchen.

- **OPEN:** All year, except Christmas
- **ROOMS:** Six rooms, five en suite
- **PRICE:** €27-30 per person sharing. Single €35

- **NOTES:**
No credit cards accepted.
Dinner 6.30pm, €20, separate tables. Bring your own wine. No wheelchair access.
Children welcome. Irish spoken.

- **DIRECTIONS:**
Details of boats and planes to Aran are available in all Galway tourist offices. Peadar Poíl always meets visitors and gives you a lift up to the house (on his tractor).

RENVYLE

Ronnie Counihan
Letterfrack, Connemara
County Galway
Tel: (095) 43571, Fax: 43515
renvyle@iol.ie
www.renvyle.com

Renvyle, just about as far west as you can go, is also just about as far relaxed as the human spirit can get, an independent chill-out republic.

Some folk refer to Renvyle as 'The Kelly's of the West'. That's not quite right. Kelly's is smarter and more polished, where Renvyle is calmer and more sedate than the Wexford icon, but the two definitely share a chill-out code which is, in both cases, pretty irresistible. You walk into the old-style lobby here (and Renvyle is an interior designer's heaven: they have done little to the original template of the house, so all the old and unique style is perfectly intact), you see that blazing fire, and you just want to crash out, like now! It's a potent mix of hospitality and ambience, and Ronnie Counihan and his team stoke it just right, with staff who are young, charming and unpretentious, all in the spirit of the place. In the kitchen, Tim O'Sullivan has a good crew, and the cooking has real soul, making for a great dining room with, take note, a pianist who plays some fine Chopin.

● **OPEN:** Feb-Dec
● **ROOMS:** 68 rooms
● **PRICE:** €95 per person sharing. Single supplement €32. Look out for frequent offers - see website.

● **NOTES:**
All major cards accepted. Restaurant, serving dinner 7pm-9.30pm, €40. Children welcome, many facilities. Full wheelchair access.

● **DIRECTIONS:**
The hotel is signposted from Kylemore. At Letterfrack, turn right, and travel four miles, until you see the hotel gates.

SEAMIST HOUSE

Sheila Griffin
Clifden, Connemara
County Galway
Tel: (095) 21441
sgriffin@eircom.net
www.connemara.net/seaview

Sheila Griffin brings animated
bohemian energy to this great
B&B: just the right address
for a few days way out west.

The animated way in which Sheila Griffin talks about the
'energy' she tries to bring to her lovely house is the key
to the success of this great Clifden getaway. Others
understand feng shui as a pair of wacky words: Ms Griffin
understands the concept as the need for a room to have
positive energy from furnishings and colour, light and
shade, comfort and contrast, and she also understands
her own role as hostess as demanding that she bring her
own energy to her house. This she does in spades:
whistling up some pancakes with a compote of winter
berries and some crème fraîche in the blink of an eye,
planning a different daily special breakfast dish, always
reassessing her rooms to make them better, more
comfortable. Seamist is a great house, and if you are
planning a visit to Stefan Matz's new restaurant, then this
would be our choice of address for a Clifden escapade.

- **OPEN:** All year, except Christmas
- **ROOMS:** Six rooms, all en suite
- **PRICE:** €32-42 per person sharing

- **NOTES:**
Visa, Mastercard. No dinner.
No wheelchair access.
No facilities for children.
Street parking just outside.

- **DIRECTIONS:**
Right beside the Bank of Ireland in the centre of
Clifden. Clifden is approximately 1 hour's drive from
Galway city.

ALLO'S TOWNHOUSE

Armel Whyte & Helen Mullane
41 Church Street
Listowel
County Kerry
Tel: (068) 22880 Fax: 22803
www.allos.ie

Comfortable rooms, comforting food, calm hospitality and delightful design are the alluring and stylish template of the truly lovely Allo's Townhouse.

Anyone who has followed the careers of Helen Mullane and Armel Whyte has always appreciated that this team have a special, exacting eye when it comes to design, a cultured gaze which manages to make a space seem just right. Study the design of the three rooms in Allo's Townhouse, right in the centre of Listowel, and you see how that cultured gaze has been put to work to make rooms that are, first and foremost, comfortable, and yet where the design elements are always used to feed into that comfort, creating welcoming beds, superb bathrooms, an air of languor and classical comfort. It's a beautifully realised piece of design, and as such it is all of a piece with this gorgeous pub, where you will enjoy gorgeous, precise breakfasts in the bistro, fabulous food at lunchtime in the beautiful bar, and great cooking from Theo and his team at dinner. Allo's has about all you need.

- **OPEN:** All year. Closed Sun & Mon
- **ROOMS:** Three rooms, all en suite
- **PRICE:** €50 p.p.s. Single supplement €13

- **NOTES:**
Dinner and bar food served in Allo's Bar & Bistro.
No wheelchair access.
Children welcome.

- **DIRECTIONS:**
1 hour's drive from Limerick on the N69.
Allo's Townhouse is in the centre of Listowel, on the one-way system. You will find it opposite the main Garda station.

THE CAPTAIN'S HOUSE

Jim & Mary Milhench
The Mall, Dingle
County Kerry
Tel: (066) 915 1531, Fax: 915 1079
captigh@eircom.net
homepage.eircom.net/~captigh/

Good fun, good food, good value and good hospitality are the quartet of charms that make Jim and Mary's house such a staple of busy Dingle.

Unpretentious and welcoming, the Captain's House is a friendly, fun destination, with just the right spirit of adventure and exploration to suit a bubbly town like Dingle. Jim Milhench was a seafaring man before he met Mary, and his nautical background explains how this landlocked house, right smack in the centre of Dingle – and with a front garden dissected by the river – gets its unusual name. Mind you, it could have been Riverrun.
The intimacy of the bedrooms and the superb housekeeping make for a house that oozes comfort, and that comfort is further congratulated by the splendour of the cooking and the baking – whatever you do, don't pass on the porter cake, offered to all guests with tea when they arrive, for it is a rich, boozy, beautiful concoction, and the care taken with the porter cake is echoed by some really excellent breakfasts featuring excellent local foods.

● **OPEN:** 15 Mar-15 Nov
● **ROOMS:** Eight rooms, one suite, all en suite
● **PRICE:** €45-€50 per person sharing. Single rate €55, Suite €60 per person sharing

● **NOTES:**
Visa, Mastercard accepted.
No meals. No smoking house. No wheelchair access.
No facilities for children.

● **DIRECTIONS:**
Follow signs to Dingle town centre. The Captain's House is 200m on the left, after the first big roundabout.

EMLAGH HOUSE

Michael & Marion Kavanagh
Dingle
County Kerry
Tel: (066) 915 2345, Fax: 915 2369
info@emlaghhouse.com
www.emlaghhouse.com

A country house in the grand style, Emlagh is luxurious and thoughtful, a great destination for fun times in Dingle, and touring the peninsula.

Emla? Or Emlee? The latter pronunciation, with its gentle rising vowels at the end of the name, tends to be the preferred way to sound Emlagh, and in truth it suits this comfortable, grand house, which has a distinctly feminine, gentle persuasion to its luxury.

And Emlagh is luxurious, with all the lavish points one can achieve with a purpose-built house: the underfloor heating in the bathrooms, the bedrooms with their confident capaciousness, the welcoming hallway, the fabulous etchings by Maria Simmons-Gooding which vie with many other paintings, the calm, bracing sweep of the truly lovely breakfast room with its smashing views out to the sea. There are even state-of-the-art Bose sound systems in each room! That's luxury.

Grainne and Marion Kavanagh manage Emlagh with quiet patience, and it's a brilliant destination for buzzy Dingle.

- **OPEN:** All year, except 1-28 Dec
- **ROOMS:** 10 rooms
- **PRICE:** €85-120 per person sharing, €40 single supplement

- **NOTES:**
Mastercard and Visa accepted. Light day menu with snacks served until 7pm. No smoking in bedrooms. One room fully wheelchair accessible. Private car park. Children under 8 years not encouraged.

- **DIRECTIONS:**
As one approaches Dingle, Emlagh House is the first turn left at the entrance to the town.

HAWTHORN HOUSE

Noel & Mary O'Brien
Shelbourne Street, Kenmare
County Kerry
Tel: (064) 41035, Fax: 41932
info@hawthornhousekenmare.con
www.hawthornhousekenmare.con

Mary O'Brien's restless renovations keep the pretty Hawthorn House on a par with the stratospheric standards that are characteristic of Kenmare.

Hawthorn is such a pretty B&B, with such a fantastic location – right smack in the centre of lovely Kenmare town – that Mary O'Brien could have simply sat back, when she bought the house several years back, secure in the knowledge that guests would turn up looking for accommodation each and every year.

But, that is not the Kenmare way, for the natives of this town set standards, and then, each and every year, they seek to better them. So, Mrs O'Brien has been installing the power showers which are now de rigeur, she has been redecorating, she has been enlarging the rooms, all the better to ensure that Hawthorn stays up to the mark and up to the minute. This animated energy and determination is the spirit of this capable woman, and it makes for a splendid B&B, a lovely house which offers excellent comfort and very excellent value for money.

- **OPEN:** All year, except Christmas
- **ROOMS:** Eight rooms, en suite
- **PRICE:** €35 per person sharing, Single occupancy €45

- **NOTES:**
Visa and Mastercard accepted. No dinner. No wheel-chair access. Enclosed private parking. Children welcome, babysitting available.

- **DIRECTIONS:**
There are three main streets in Kenmare. Hawthorn House is situated on Shelbourne Street, the quieter of the three.

10 PLACES FOR
GREAT ROMANCE

DOLPHIN BEACH
CLIFDEN, Co GALWAY

ECHO LODGE
BALLINGARRY, Co LIMERICK

ISKEROON
BUNAVALLA, Co KERRY

QUAY HOUSE
CLIFDEN, Co GALWAY

RATHCOURSEY
MIDLETON, Co CORK

RENVYLE HOUSE
LETTERFRACK, Co GALWAY

SHEEN FALLS LODGE
KENMARE, Co KERRY

TODDIES
KINSALE, Co CORK

WINEPORT LODGE
ATHLONE, Co WESTMEATH

ZUNI
KILKENNY, Co KILKENNY

ISKEROON

Geraldine Burkitt & David Hare
Bunavalla, Caherdaniel
County Kerry
Tel: (066) 947 5119, Fax: 947 5488
info@iskeroon.com
www.iskeroon.com

Drop-dead gorgeous, and
now world-famous,
Iskeroon is uniquely
beautiful and truly special.

It had to happen, and it has happened. Iskeroon, that
beacon of utterly remote loveliness on the coast of
Kerry, is the only destination in Ireland listed in 'The
Hotel Book: Great Escapes Europe'. One of only 48 of the
'most stylish' places to stay in Europe, David and
Geraldine's gorgeous house is in there along with Reid's
Palace in Madeira, the Ice Hotel in Sweden and the
Cipriani in Venice. Apres ça, le deluge.

David and Geraldine can handle this sort of acclaim, no
problem. They are individualists, people with expert,
patient skill at creating and maximising the shocking
beauty of their house. To be honest, the Reids and
Ciprianis of this world are lucky to be classed with
Iskeroon, for this is a house to take your breath away,
both for its staggering location, and its sheer beauty. Even
just once, you really should stay here: you're worth it.

- **OPEN:** 1 May-30 Sep
- **ROOMS:** Three rooms, each with private bathroom.
Self-catering apartment for two
- **PRICE:** €55 per person sharing. Single supplement
€25

- **NOTES:**
Visa, Mastercard accepted. Light supper available Mon-Fri, if
pre booked, 8pm, €25. No wheelchairs. No children.

- **DIRECTIONS:**
Find the Scarriff Inn between Waterville and Caherdaniel.
Take sign to Bunavalla Pier. At the pier, go through gate
marked 'private road', beside beach through pillars.

THE KILLARNEY PARK HOTEL

Padraig & Janet Treacy
Kenmare Place, Killarney
County Kerry
Tel: (064) 35555, Fax: 35266
info@killarneyparkhotel.ie
www.killarneyparkhotel.ie

Is the Killarney Park the best-run hotel in Ireland? Very, very likely: it's a peach of a place, and a real star.

The Killarney Park makes you feel good, and makes your heart feel glad. This pretty hotel is so well run by manager Donagh Davern, and the staff are so charming and hospitable, that we would reckon this is the best-run hotel in Ireland at this moment in time.

The service isn't 5-star formal: it's simply courteous, polite and there when you need it. The rooms are comfortable, the cooking in the restaurant is superb, and the food in the bar is surpassing: this is where all the smart folk in Killarney eat at lunchtime, and it is a brilliant place to feed the kids in the early evening. The housekeeping is second-to-none, the atmosphere serene, ennobling. Above all, this is the hotel of your dreams, a place of proud professionalism, of Irish hospitality, a place that wants to be as good as it can possibly be. They are reaching for the stars in the KP.

- **OPEN:** All year, except Christmas
- **ROOMS:** 71 rooms
- **PRICE:** €240-€360 per room

- **NOTES:**
Visa, Mastercard, Amex, Laser. Restaurant & Bar open daily, Dinner €50. Recommended for vegetarians. Children welcome, babysitting and facilities available on request. Full wheelchair access.

- **DIRECTIONS:**
At 1st roundabout in Killarney (coming from Cork), take 1st exit for town centre. At 2nd roundabout take 2nd exit and at 3rd roundabout take 1st exit.

THE PARK HOTEL

Francis & John Brennan
Kenmare
County Kerry
Tel: (064) 41200, Fax: 41402
info@parkkenmare.com
www.parkkenmare.com

A glam new spa is planned
for the autumn but, thanks
to Francis Brennan, The Park
already overflows with TLC.

They are already getting mighty excited in The Park about
Sámas, the glam spa which is scheduled to open in
Autumn 2003. Designed by Opperman Associates, who
have developed spas in many glitzy resorts, with E'SPA as
the spa consultants, it is all a sure sign that Francis
Brennan is aiming once again to raise the bar regarding
our expectations of what a great hotel should offer.
But then, Mr Brennan has been doing that for many years
now, and doing it principally through his own
embodiment of what a great hotel host should be. To be
honest, if Francis Brennan ran a two-bed dive in a Nissen
hut on a housing estate in north Limerick city, you would
still clamour to get into it. This man is the greatest
hotelier of his generation, and his creation of
international standards both in The Park Hotel and in the
lovely town of Kenmare are unmatched by anyone else.

- **OPEN:** 18 Apr-30 Nov & 23 Dec-2 Jan
- **ROOMS:** 46 rooms
- **PRICE:** €366 per person sharing, B&B

- **NOTES:**
All major cards accepted. Restaurant open daily,
Dinner from 7pm, €64.
Full wheelchair access.
Secure parking. Private dining if required. Restaurant
available to 8pm for under 6 year olds. Spa opens this
year.

- **DIRECTIONS:**
At the top of Kenmare town.

PARKNASILLA

Jim Feeney
Sneem
County Kerry
Tel: (064) 45122, Fax: 45323
res@parknasilla-gsh.com
www.greatsouthernhotels.com

Parknasilla is one of the great chill-out zones, thanks to great staff, a gorgeouslocation, and a fabulous collection of modern Irish paintings.

At some point in the future, some report by some bureaucrats will recommend to the Government that the state has no business running hotels, and that the Great Southern Hotel group – which has Parknasilla as its shining star – should be put up for sale. And the Government, counting its cents as usual, will agree, and a century of distinguished, cultured hospitality will be put out to the highest bidder.

Let's imagine another way of looking at it that doesn't exclude everything but the bottom line. Should the Government control an organisation which can train people in hospitality, which can show those same people how to work in and appreciate the culture of hospitality which we Irish are supposed to hold so dear? Is that not a valuable project? Because Parknasilla and its dedicated team do things so well, and deserve our appreciation.

● **OPEN:** All year
● **ROOMS:** 84 rooms
● **PRICE:** €126-€165 per person sharing. Single supplement €26. Look out for frequent offers.

● **NOTES:**
All major cards accepted. Wheelchair access.
Children welcome, beach, swimming pool, walks. Special rates available for 3-5 day's stay, full board, and good value.

● **DIRECTIONS:**
15 miles from Kenmare, 3 miles from Sneem. Travel on the N70 (Ring of Kerry) and you will see their sign.

SHEEN FALLS LODGE

Adriaan Bartels
Kenmare
County Kerry
Tel: (064) 41600, Fax: 41386
info@sheenfallslodge.ie
www.sheenfallslodge.ie

The Sheen Falls is on a roll these days, with cooking and service from a brilliant team hitting the heights of the sublime.

Do you know what it is that makes the SFL work, the thing that powers it along and makes it a truly special place? It's not the grandness, though it sure is grand. It's not the location, though the location is truly fantastic. No, what powers this stylish, comfortable hotel along and sets it apart is the commitment of the team who work here. You genuinely get a sense of people determined to do their job just as well as it can be done, people who would in no way be happy to just go through the motions and do that 5-star service thing by the book.

Manager Adriaan Bartels leads his team from the front, whilst chef Chris Farrell leads his kitchen team from the front, and the conjunction of service and food is done with true élan and understanding. Indeed, the cooking in the SFL goes from strength to strength, but then you can say the same of every aspect of this distinguished hotel.

● **OPEN:** First Fri in Feb-2 Jan
● **ROOMS:** 66 rooms
● **PRICE:** €260-€395 per standard room. Supplements apply for superior rooms and suites

● **NOTES:**
All major cards accepted. Recommended for vegetarians. Full wheelchair access. Children welcome, babysitting, cots, outdoor play area 'kiddies club'. Two thatched cottages for rental, exclusively catered for.

● **DIRECTIONS:**
Heading towards Glengarriff, the hotel is on the first turn left after the suspension bridge.

SHELBURNE LODGE

Tom & Maura Foley O'Connell
Killowen
Cork Road
Kenmare
County Kerry
Tel: (064) 41013, Fax: 42135

Maura Foley is the style lovers' style lover, and Shelburne is a magnificent tribute to her extraordinary design talents. *icon*

'It's fantastic what it does to a room,' Maura Foley will say about her use of large mirrors in the rooms and bathrooms of Shelburne Lodge. 'But it must reflect something: when you look into it there must be a picture'.

There you have it. In Shelburne, perhaps the style lover's icon destination, Maura Foley looks at every space, every thoroughfare, every room, every reflection, so that there is a complete picture. If you wanted to know how someone can be such a triumphantly distinctive mistress of style, that quote explains everything: don't just think of the mirror, think of what the mirror is reflecting. Think of the picture. The big picture. The little picture. Every picture. Everything about this magnificent house – the colours, furniture, paintings – is sublime, an elegant conspiracy of the very best good taste. And breakfasts are magnificent.

- **OPEN:** 1 Apr-30 Oct
- **ROOMS:** Seven rooms, all en suite
- **PRICE:** €110-€130 per room. Single €70-€80

- **NOTES:**
No dinner (good restaurants locally).
Enclosed car parking.
No wheelchair access.
Children welcome, high chair, cot.

- **DIRECTIONS:**
300m from Kenmare, across from the golf course on the Cork road. Kenmare is 35 miles from Kerry airport, 60 miles from Cork airport.

ZUNI

**Paul & Paula Byrne, Sandra &
Alan McDonald
26 Patrick Street, Kilkenny city
Tel: (056) 772 3999
Fax: 775 6400
info@zuni.ie www.zuni.ie**

Zuni is as smart as it gets:
smart dining room, smart
bar, smart rooms, smart
people. That's a lot of smarts.

Zuni, Kilkenny's smash bang! success story, is one of the
smartest places we have come across in recent years. The
cooking is great, the public spaces are dead glam, the staff
are personable and efficient, the value for money is
exceptional, and the rooms are excellent. How did this
quartet – two husband-and-wife crews – manage to make
it all look so ridiculously simple? How did they so
effortlessly ride out the crucial matter of a change of
kitchen team? How did they get the design so right, so
that you can eat here for a business dinner or a big slap-
up! party and enjoy the room either way? Students of the
business should take a close look at Zuni, for it is as
smart an operation as has been created since the days of
Roly's Bistro. All we know is that we – and everyone else
we know – are always happy to be walking one more time
through these doors. A brilliant, smart, hip place.

- **OPEN:** All year, except Christmas
- **ROOMS:** 13 rooms, all en suite
- **PRICE:** €50-€80 per person sharing

- **NOTES:**
 Visa, Mastercard, Amex, Laser. Restaurant open for
dinner Mon-Sun. Full wheelchair access. Enclosed private
parking at rear. Children welcome, under 7s welcome in
restaurant before 7pm.

- **DIRECTIONS:**
Located in the city centre, on Patrick Street, which is
round the corner from Kilkenny Castle. Take M50 from
Dublin airport. Take N7 south bound direct to Kilkenny.

IVYLEIGH HOUSE

Dinah & Jerry Campion
Bank Place
Portlaoise, County Laois
Tel: (0502) 22081, Fax: 63343
ivyleigh@gofree.indigo.ie
www.ivyleigh.com

There isn't an unconsidered detail in Dinah Campion's exemplary B&B, a destination with stratospheric standards that make the heart sing.

A lady from the tourist authorities once told Dinah Campion, before she opened her meticulous house to guests, that a top-flight B&B would never work in Portlaoise. The lady hadn't reckoned on the determined Mrs Campion, and she hadn't reckoned on the fact that when word spreads of someone who does a job as well as it can be done, that word of mouth will very soon ensure that you have a roaring success on your hands. Ivyleigh is a roaring success, because Mrs Campion does her job as well as it can be done. The extraordinary housekeeping, the superb, fresh breakfasts, the intense comfort of the rooms, where every detail is chosen with such care, this is B&B keeping as an art form. Breakfast, amidst many highlights, is one of the very best. 'A fried breakfast must be cooked from the pan,' Mrs Campion asserts, correctly, and that questing care defines Ivyleigh.

- **OPEN:** All year
- **ROOMS:** Four rooms, all en suite
- **PRICE:** €110 double room, twin room €55 per person sharing. Single in double/twin €70, single room €60

- **NOTES:**
No dinner. No wheelchair access. On street car parking. Children over 8 years welcome.

- **DIRECTIONS:**
Approaching from Dublin direction, turn off M7 for Portlaoise, turn right at Church (sign for railway station) and left at next junction for 200yds and keep right at next junction. Ivyleigh House is 30yds on right hand side.

PRESTON HOUSE

Allison & Michael Dowling
Main Street
Abbeyleix
County Laois
Tel: (0502) 31432
Fax: (0502) 31432

Preston House is a beautiful old schoolhouse in the beautiful village of Abbeyleix, and a vital address for travellers on the Dublin-Cork road.

A much-loved café, with a number of cleverly designed guest rooms, Allison Dowling's lovely Preston House is one of the landmark buildings in the gorgeous heritage town of Abbeyleix.

Downstairs in the café, Mrs Dowling cooks fine, country food: smoked haddock chowder; roast sirloin of beef with Yorkshire pudding; a warm salad of the delicious Rudd's ham, a speciality from County Offaly; a good vegetarian lasagne; excellent old-style desserts such as apple and blueberry crumble. The café enjoys an ageless ambience, enhanced by the fact that they even serve wine with a paper napkin tucked around the neck of the bottle.

The rooms are ingeniously designed, and very, very comfortable, as are the public rooms reserved for visitors. And the location, on the busy N7/N8 Dublin-Cork road, makes Preston a vital stop-over destination.

● **OPEN:** All year (except 10 days at Christmas) Closed Mondays
● **ROOMS:** Four double rooms, all en suite
● **PRICE:** €80 double room, €45 single room

● **NOTES:**
All major cards accepted. Café open lunch Tue-Sun, and dinner, €35, Thurs-Sat. Reservations recommended. No wheelchair access. No smoking. Children welcome, high chair, cot. Car park at rear.

● **DIRECTIONS:**
Large ivy-clad school house on the main street in Abbeyleix (the Dublin/Cork Road).

ROUNDWOOD HOUSE

Frank & Rosemary Kennan
Mountrath
County Laois
Tel: (0502) 32120, Fax: 32711
roundwood@eircom.net
hidden-ireland.com/roundwood

Roundwood is loveable: simple as that. If you can somehow resist Frank and Rosemary Kennan's charming house, then you simply have no heart.

Abandon all critical perspective, ye who enter herein. Roundwood is not a house to be cool about. It's not a house to be indifferent about. It's simply a place to fall in love with, whatever your age, sex, nationality or shoe size. If you have any size of a heart at all – even a heart that is a size or two too small, like the Grinch – you will fall under Roundwood's spell, the Grinch in you will be excised, and you will be enthusing to all your new best friends, as you sit and chat and drink around the dinner table, about what an amazing place this is.

The cold eye which you might cast about the place, and which might remark on the ancien pauvre style and the elegantly distressed furnishings, will be dissolved in the delight of Rosemary's splendid cooking, and the irresistible bonhommie this lovely house seem to conjure from out of the ether. What an amazing enchantment!

- **OPEN:** All year, except Christmas Day
- **ROOMS:** 10 rooms, all with private bathrooms
- **PRICE:** €70 per person sharing. Single supplement €25

- **NOTES:**
Dinner, 8.30pm, €45, communal table.
Book by noon.
No wheelchair access.
Children welcome, high chair, cot, babysitting.

- **DIRECTIONS:**
Turn right at T-junction in Mountrath for Ballyfin, then left onto R440. Travel for 5km on the R440 until you come to the house.

HOLLYWELL COUNTRY HOUSE

Rosaleen & Tom Maher
Liberty Hill
Carrick-on-Shannon
County Leitrim
Tel & Fax: (078) 21124
hollywell@esat.biz.com

You read it here first: they are gone mad foodie in Leitrim, with cosmopolitan cooking operations sprouting up here and there: a new mid-west Manhattan.

Things in and around Carrick are 'bucking up considerably', says Tom Maher. How so? Well, Mr Maher's sons have taken over a pub called The Oarsman, where they are serving some cracking food. There is a new Indonesian restaurant in Keshcarrigan. The Egyptian restaurant has relocated to Jamestown and is now called Al Mezze, and a German-owned restaurant in Cootehill bridge is proving to be very consistent.

Blimey! The area is becoming as cosmopolitan and as foodie as Manhattan. What a transformation from what was, as Mr Maher says himself, 'a culinary desert'. Mr Maher is too hard on himself, because whilst there may have been few places to eat around Carrick, there has always been Hollywell, and Hollywell has always been a beacon of civilised hospitality, of stylish cooking, of comfort. It's a lovely house, a truly pioneering destination.

- **OPEN:** 2 Jan-20 Dec
- **ROOMS:** Four rooms, all en suite
- **PRICE:** €46-€53 per person sharing. Single €50-€60

- **NOTES:**
No dinner.
Enclosed car park.
No wheelchair access.
Children over 12 years welcome.

- **DIRECTIONS:**
From Carrick-on-Shannon, cross the bridge, keep left at Gings pub. The entrance to Hollywell is on the left.

BALLYTEIGUE HOUSE

Richard & Margaret Johnson
Rockhill, Bruree
County Limerick
Tel & Fax: (063) 90575
ballyteigue@eircom.net
homepage.eircom.net/~ballyteigue/

north
east
west
south

Margaret Johnson's hospitality is maternal, mothering, magnificent, just the right aura for this fine farmhouse smack on the Cork-Limerick border.

Get back to Ballyteigue after an evening out, walk up the stairs of this ruggedly handsome old farmhouse, open your door, get ready for bed, pull back the blanket, tuckle up, and let the heat of that electric blanket course through your body like a great big hug! Ah, having someone switch on your electric blanket for when you get back home: is that not a definition of everything that luxury and hospitality is all about?!

Margaret Johnson is a formidable woman, gifted, capable, and the most marvellous host and conversationalist. When you stay at this sweet old farmhouse, you are taken into her care, and there you stay, like a little child, being mothered into relaxation and happiness, fed tea and banana bread, and good breakfasts, and all the things your heart desires, especially someone to plug in your electric blanket at night-time when you are out at play. Bliss!

● **OPEN:** Throughout summer, winter months by arrangement, closed Christmas and New Year
● **ROOMS:** Five rooms, one twin, three double, one single
● **PRICE:** €35 per person sharing, B&B

● **NOTES:**
Visa, Mastercard. Dinner by request only, set menu discussed, €25. No wheelchair access. Secure parking. Supervised children welcome (note there is a garden pond).

● **DIRECTIONS:**
Pass O'Rourke's Cross (filling station on left) take next right, where you will see first finger sign for house.

THE MUSTARD SEED

Daniel Mullane
Echo Lodge, Ballingarry
County Limerick
Tel: (069) 68508, Fax: 68511
mustard@indigo.ie
www.mustardseed.ie

Dan Mullane is not just the master of hospitality: he is also the master of original interior design.

Dan Mullane can make perfect spaces. Like some of the other design classics in this book – Buggy's, Quay House, Rathcoursey – The Mustard Seed is the work of a man whose skill and passion for design leads to a style which is utterly unique: no one else makes spaces like Mr Mullane, and you can't believe that anyone else could.

He could wing it on style alone, especially with the new suites which should be awarded every prize going, but Mr Mullane congratulates his design skills with a wry, witty hospitality that is the icing on this fabulous cake. Backed by a devoted team, Mr Mullane's hospitality animates and unifies the beautiful Echo Lodge, creating one of the most distinct destinations anywhere in Ireland. Comfort is all: comfortable rooms, comfort cooking, comforting hospitality, all of it quietly and confidently world-class in every detail. Buddha is in the detail: Mr Mullane knows it.

- **OPEN:** All year
- **ROOMS:** 16 rooms, including three suites
- **PRICE:** €86-€140 p.p.s. Single supplement €30, triple room supplement €60

- **NOTES:**
Dinner in their restaurant, €48. Give advance notice for special diets. Full wheelchair access. House not suitable for young children.

- **DIRECTIONS:**
At the top of Adare village, take the Killarney road for quarter mile, until you reach the first turning off to the left, signed for Ballingarry.

GHAN HOUSE

Paul Carroll
Carlingford
County Louth
Tel: (042) 937 3682, Fax: 937 3772
ghanhouse@eircom.net
www.ghanhouse.com

The Carroll family's Ghan House is a tearaway success story, and a model of professional, polite service.

Paul Carroll has always impressed as a young man with a very clear vision of what he wanted to achieve with Ghan House. As time has gone by, as this pretty house just on the edge of beautiful Carlingford village has developed, focused, gotten better and better and more and more popular, it is clear that his plan to create one of the great resort escapes has succeeded: everyone, from North and South, loves to get away to Ghan.

The house itself, a low-set Georgian house whose style is rare in Ireland, and the adjacent annex, are relaxed places, and they form the perfect base for getting the most out of the village, with its eclectic mixture of restaurants and pubs. But Ghan itself is a destination restaurant address, with superb cooking that is hugely enjoyable, and in addition to their occasional gourmet nights, they now also stage Georgian banquets. Ghan is one hot ticket.

- **OPEN:** All year, except 23 Dec-15 Jan
- **ROOMS:** 12 bedrooms, all en suite
- **PRICE:** €75 per person sharing

- **NOTES:**
Visa, Mastercard, Laser, Amex. Restaurant open Fri-Sat, 7pm-9.30pm. Midweek & Sun by arrangement, €45. No wheelchair access. Telephone first to discuss policy on children.

- **DIRECTIONS:**
Approaching from south, Ghan House is 1st driveway on left after 30mph sign on entering Carlingford. 53 miles from Dublin, 43 miles from Belfast.

NEWPORT HOUSE

Kieran & Thelma Thompson
Newport
County Mayo
Tel: (098) 41222, Fax: 41613
info@newporthouse.ie
www.newporthouse.ie

Newport House is really an
independent republic:
sumptuous, exquisite, heady,
decadent, desirable.

'I have a lovely menu for you this evening, sir.' 'I hope you have a lovely stay, pet.' Is there anyone better at the business of hospitality than Catherine, the magical mistress of Kieran and Thelma Thompson's beautiful country house? And could there be a more appropriate house in which to see someone display such magisterial control and character? We could just watch and listen to this lady all evening, as she shepherds her contented customers through the evening, doing everything from meeting and greeting to drinks to wine service, checking that you have everything you need. She is a true star, and her energy animates Newport and makes it one of the very finest of Ireland's country houses.

Mind you, everyone else plays just as hard as Catherine. John Gavan's cooking is superb, the rooms are pristine, the attention to detail second to none. A magical place.

- **OPEN:** 19 Mar-6Oct
- **ROOMS:** 18 rooms, all en suite
- **PRICE:** Low season €104-€130, High season €112-€138. Single supplement €24, superior room supplement €22

- **NOTES:**
All major credit cards accepted.
Restaurant open for casual lunch and formal dinner.
Dinner €50.
Limited wheelchair access.
Children very welcome. Secure parking.

- **DIRECTIONS:**
In the centre of the village of Newport, on N59 route.

10 PLACES GREAT
FOR WEEKENDS

ASSOLAS HOUSE
KANTURK, Co CORK

BALLYKNOCKEN HOUSE
ASHFORD, Co WICKLOW

BROOK LODGE INN
MACREDDIN, Co WICKLOW

CASTLEMURRAY HOUSE
DUNKINEELY, Co DONEGAL

GHAN HOUSE
CARLINGFORD, Co LOUTH

KILGRANEY
BAGENALSTOWN, Co CARLOW

LONGUEVILLE HOUSE
MALLOW, Co CORK

MACNEAN HOUSE
BLACKLION, Co CAVAN

RENVYLE
LETTERFRACK, Co GALWAY

SEAMIST HOUSE
CLIFDEN, Co GALWAY

ROSTURK WOODS

Louisa & Alan Stoney
Mulrany, Westport
County Mayo
Tel & Fax: (098) 36264
stoney@iol.ie
www.rosturk-woods.com

A beautiful house in an awesomely beautiful part of Mayo, Rosturk has that wild, westerly spirit in spades, thanks to Louisa Stoney's energy.

Rosturk is a lovely house, brightly coloured and gaily decorated, tucked away in the woods, and, above all, a place blessed with the light that bounces off the nearby Clew Bay, a light that suffuses and animates this lovely place. Something about this house seems perfectly to capture and express the wild, western spirit of this adorable part of Mayo, on the road between Newport and Achill Island. But, if the house expresses a spirit of place, Louisa Stoney trumps it, every time. For here is one of those extraordinary women who manage to do all, and do it charmingly and effortlessly, and whose animation brings alive the place where they live and work. She is a true hostess; super knowledgeable about the area – this year she will be suggesting you try the Linenmill restaurant in Westport – a super cook should you ask for dinner, a great free spirit who makes you feel very special.

- **OPEN:** Mar-Nov
- **ROOMS:** Three double/twin rooms, all en suite
- **PRICE:** €45 per person sharing

- **NOTES:**
No credit cards accepted. Dinner, €30-€35. Full wheelchair access in self-catering accommodation. Secure parking. Children welcome, babysitting by arrangement, cot, highchair, toys.

- **DIRECTIONS:**
7 miles from Newport, heading towards Achill, after you have crossed Owengrave River, look for blue sign with Rosturk Woods. Turn left towards the sea.

THE OLD WORKHOUSE

Niamh Colgan
Ballinlough
Dunshaughlin
County Meath
Tel & Fax: (01) 825 9251
comfort@a-vip.com

Legendary breakfasts and legendary hospitality are the animus of Niamh Colgan's Old Workhouse, an ideal stop for anyone using the airport.

A guest once left their credit cards behind in The Old Workhouse, then rang from the airport, in a panic, as you might expect. Not a bother: Niamh Colgan just jumped into the car, and was at the airport 15 minutes later to rescue the forgetful traveller/guest.

So, Mrs Colgan can drive a speedy motor car, that's for sure, but this little story tells an awful lot about the sort of true, patient, gentle and resourceful care and hospitality which is Mrs Colgan's métier. She loves to look after people, beginning with breakfast, a meal into which she pours all her TLC: hot griddle cakes cooked on the Aga; buttery croissants; pears poached in sugar syrup with cardamom; bananas in lime and orange zest; poached nectarines and peaches; her own splendid granola. This isn't breakfast: this is a feast, and The Old Workhouse is a feast for all the senses for the forgetful, weary traveller.

- **OPEN:** 15 Jan-15 Dec
- **ROOMS:** Five rooms (1 mini suite, 1 superking, 2 double, 1 twin, all en suite or with private bathroom)
- **PRICE:** €55-€80 per person sharing, Single €70-€90

- **NOTES:**
Visa, Mastercard.
Wheelchair access to ground floor rooms.
Children welcome, but no reduction in price.

- **DIRECTIONS:**
On the main N3, Dublin/Cavan road.
One mile on the Dublin side of Dunshaughlin.

HILTON PARK

Johnny & Lucy Madden
Clones
County Monaghan
Tel: (047) 56007, Fax: 56033
mail@hiltonpark.ie
www.hiltonpark.ie

Wit, hospitality, and charm
are what Johnny and Lucy
Madden bring to hulkingly
handsome Hilton Park.

Johnny and Lucy Madden are witty people, folk who underplay their clever, delighting charm, only letting it escape in moments when you might almost miss it. It makes them great hosts, and great fun, and their droll humour manages to corral this monstrously enormous house, and bring it someplace close to earth.

Like all those folk blessed – or perhaps doomed - to inherit an ancestral pile, they work endlessly at the house. The imaginative pleasure gardens work which they carried out almost a decade ago has now matured beautifully, and they have achieved a major refurbishment of the grand drawing room. Meantime – is there ever a meantime in a house like this? – they have also renovated the gatelodge, which has been a great success for those who want to escape to a spot of self-catering. Personally, we wouldn't miss this great house, and its great cooking.

● **OPEN:** Apr-Sep and year round for block bookings
● **ROOMS:** Six rooms, all en suite
● **PRICE:** €110 per person sharing, B&B

● **NOTES:**
Visa, Mastercard. Dinner, 8pm (8.30pm Fridays), €45, book ahead. No wheelchair access.
Secure parking.
Not suitable for children under 8 years.

● **DIRECTIONS:**
77 miles from Dublin. Take N3 to Cavan, Cavan by-pass, leave at 2nd junction, go through Ballyhaise and Scotshouse and Hilton is next entry on left, after golf club.

COOPERSHILL HOUSE

Brian & Lindy O'Hara
Riverstown
County Sligo
Tel: (071)9165108, Fax: 9165466
ohara@coopershill.com
www.coopershill.com

Coopershill has a welcoming, lived-in feeling, just the sort of spirit which explains why house party groups are so devoted to this beautiful house.

Some of the grander country houses can feel a little bit like museum pieces, places you should admire, but don't dare to touch. Coopershill is not like that. It is pristine, and yet its immaculate nature is not at all hands-off! Instead, the house looks and feels as if it has been deeply loved and cared for, as if it was a 225-year-old pet. It is a working house, whose métier has simply switched from being home to the O'Hara family – seven generations of them – to being a place where the O'Hara family take paying guests. And, they are very, very good indeed at the business of taking guests, thanks to Brian's wry wit and Lindy's deliciously accomplished cooking. These elements, along with the beauty of the house, perhaps explain why Coopershill is so popular with house party groups in the off season: our relatives like nothing better than to bring a tribe of mates to Riverstown for a dreamy weekend.

- **OPEN:** 1 Apr-end Oct
- **ROOMS:** Three superior and five standard rooms
- **PRICE:** €78-99 per person sharing. Single supplement €19

- **NOTES:**
Visa, Mastercard, Amex. Dinner, 8.30pm, €40-45. Children welcome, babysitting with prior notice. No wheelchair access.

- **DIRECTIONS:**
Clearly signposted from Drumfin crossroads, which is 11 miles south east of Sligo town, on route N4 towards Dublin.

CROMLEACH LODGE

Christy & Moira Tighe
Castlebaldwin, via Boyle
County Sligo
Tel: (071) 9165155, Fax: 9165455
info@cromleach.com
www.cromleach.com

Superlatively comfortable bedrooms
and original cookery from Moira
Tighe's all-women team make
Cromleach the pearl of the quarter.

Cromleach Lodge sits snugly on the hill, overlooking beautiful Lough Arrow, in south County Sligo. From a distance, it looks like a building which has sprouted new sections and extensions as the years have gone by. Inside, the style of the ground floor mixes domestic trifles in the sitting rooms with stylish professional dining rooms, whilst upstairs the bedrooms come as a brilliant surprise. Huge, super-comfortable, thoughtful and finished to a top-flight specification, they are exceptional, and the views out across the lake and the county would break your heart with delight. The next surprise, then, comes in the restaurant, where Moira Tighe's cooking is the pearl of the quarter. It's not unusual for people to describe the Cromleach menu as amongst the best food they have enjoyed in Ireland, with superb ingredients maximised by Mrs Tighe's original, feminine, intelligent style of cooking.

- **OPEN:** Feb-Nov
- **ROOMS:** 10 rooms, all en suite
- **PRICE:** €105-179 p.p.s. Single supplement €45

- **NOTES:**
All major cards accepted. Dinner €55. Wheelchair access with assistance.
Children welcome, high chair, cot, babysitting. Private family room. Recommended for vegetarians and special diets.

- **DIRECTIONS:**
Signposted from Castlebaldwin on the N4. 3 hours from Shannon airport, Dublin and Belfast.

10 PLACES
CLOSE TO DUBLIN

BALLYKNOCKEN HOUSE
ASHFORD, Co WICKLOW

BROOK LODGE INN
MACREDDIN, Co WICKLOW

KILGRANEY
BAGENALSTOWN, Co CARLOW

THE OLD WORKHOUSE
DUNSHAUGHLIN, Co MEATH

RED BANK LODGE
SKERRIES, Co DUBLIN

ROUNDWOOD HOUSE
MOUNTRATH, Co LAOIS

SALVILLE HOUSE
ENNISCORTHY, Co WEXFORD

TEMPLE SPA
MOATE, Co WESTMEATH

WINEPORT LODGE
ATHLONE, Co WESTMEATH

ZUNI
KILKENNY, Co KILKENNY

TEMPLE HOUSE

Deb & Sandy Perceval
Ballymote
County Sligo
Tel: (071) 83329, Fax: 83808
guest@templehouse.ie
www.templehouse.ie

Sandy Perceval can discover the child in all of us, which makes Temple House a great big playground for grown-ups.

Sandy Perceval can spot the child in every single one of us, and he knows exactly how to encourage that child to come out to play. 'Fancy a spin on the quad?' he asks, and if it hadn't occurred to you that, hell, yes, you sure would, then Sandy's prompting will have you in the saddle in a jiffy and tearing off around Temple House's elegant acres. It is a masterly act, done so deftly and commodiously, and no one can resist this gentle man's genial suggestions. It all makes Temple House into a place where adults can relax like kids, and to see the cat-like languor that falls over people after a day or two here is a delight: the carapace of civility drops, and we are all innocent again. Deb Perceval's excellent cooking is another bewitching element of the Temple House tapestry, and together this couple run one of the most beloved of country houses. So, go on, saddle up that quad, listen to your inner child.

- **OPEN:** 1 Apr-30 Nov
- **ROOMS:** Six rooms
- **PRICE:** €60-65 p.p.s. Single supplement €15

- **NOTES:**
Visa, Mastercard, Amex accepted. Dinner 7.30pm €30.
High tea for children under 7, 6.30pm €4-6.
No wheelchair access. Private parking. Children
welcome, rocking horse.
*Important Note: Host is very allergic to scented products.
Ask for details before booking.*

- **DIRECTIONS:**
Signposted off the N17 10km south of the N4 junction.

INCH HOUSE

John & Nora Egan
Thurles
County Tipperary
Tel: (0504) 51261/51348
Fax: 51754   inchhse@iol.ie
www.inch/house.com

Vacationers, weekenders, and locals all love Nora and John Egan's Inch House, the destination address for staying and eating in Thurles.

Nora Egan's inexhaustible energy is one of the great wonders of County Tipperary, and along with her equally dynamic lieutenant, Siobhan Carr, these two mighty women powerhouse Inch House every step of the way. For weekenders and business travellers, Inch is a modest, subtle destination, with fabulously enormous rooms that allow you to chill out in style. But for locals, Inch is also a destination restaurant, and indeed it is charming, should you be travelling alone, to be able to enjoy a dining room packed with lively folk all enjoying the good, country cooking in which the house specialises.

In the morning, the dining room is quieter, and perfect for a delicious breakfast before you hit the road: crêpes with maple syrup; scrambled eggs with smoked salmon; grilled kippers; a carefully crafted Irish breakfast. The quiet style of Inch House is both enduring and quietly endearing.

- **OPEN:** All year, except Christmas
- **ROOMS:** Five rooms, all en suite
- **PRICE:** €52.50 per person sharing, Single €60

- **NOTES:**
Dinner 7pm-9.30pm Tue-Sat, €38.
No wheelchair access.
Children welcome, cot, high chair, babysitting on request.

- **DIRECTIONS:**
Four miles from Thurles on the Nenagh road.
Turn off at the Turnpike on the main N8 road, signpost Thurles.

LEGENDS TOWNHOUSE

Michael & Rosemary O'Neill
The Kiln, Cashel
County Tipperary
Tel: (062) 61292
info@legendsguesthouse.com
www.legendsguesthouse.com

An awesome location at the foot of the Rock of Cashel is just one of Legends blessings. Great cooking and fine service are also part of the parcel.

You always wanted to stay in a house that was right smack at the foot of the Rock of Cashel, so thank heavens for the lovely Legends. Michael & Rosemary O'Neill's pretty house has the most staggering location: as you eat dinner in their super restaurant, the Rock towers and lowers just out the window, awesome and inspiring.

The location – the house is also just a stone's throw off the main N8 Dublin-Cork road – is incredible, but the hospitality of the O'Neill's, and especially Mr O'Neill's measured, delicious and impressive cooking, really do lay some cherries on the icing on your cake. It is this combination of effects, underscored by some truly professional service, that makes the whole Legends experience so fine. If you want great food, a cosy room and a night away from the kids, then it's ace. If you are touring in search of your ancestors, then it's incredible.

- **OPEN:** All year, except two weeks in Nov & Feb
- **ROOMS:** Seven rooms, all en suite
- **PRICE:** €64 per person sharing

- **NOTES:**
Restaurant open for dinner Mon-Sun, €42.
No wheelchair access.
Children - family rooms, but no children under 10 years in restaurant.

- **DIRECTIONS:**
From the N8, take the R660 to Holy Cross, Legends Restaurant and Townhouse is the fourth house on the left hand side.

AN BOHREEN

Jim & Ann Mulligan
Killineen West, Dungarvan
County Waterford
Tel: (051) 291010
mulligans@anbohreen.com
www.anbohreen.com

Ann Mulligan's fabulous cooking is the star of the pretty An Bohreen, and the value for money is so amazing you can't afford to miss this new arrival.

What an unusual place. Set high on a hill with a 360-degree view encompassing sea and mountains, yet conveniently close to the N25, this 2-year-old B&B looks, at first, rather conventional. It's a tidy modern home, decorated in pastel shades, and its four en suite rooms are rather characterless. But wait: owners Jim and Ann Mulligan have something great in store for you: namely the cuisine. Ann, an American graduate of the Ballymaloe Cookery School, serves dinner with 24 hours' notice. And it's supreme down to the last detail: tasty cream of celeriac soup with home-made honey-nut bread; green salad; luscious local lamb chops with mint sauce and roasted salmon with champ, followed by a beyond-sinful chocolate marquise, a multi-layered creation of buttery cake sandwiched between slabs of chocolate and mocha buttercream. Breakfast is sublime, the value is amazing.

- **OPEN:** Mar 17-end Oct
- **ROOMS:** Four rooms
- **PRICE:** €32-€34 per person sharing. Single rate €46-€49

- **NOTES:**
Visa, Mastercard, Amex. Dinner 7pm, €30, book by noon. No wheelchair access. Secure parking.

- **DIRECTIONS:**
Travelling from Waterford on the N25, after the town of Lemybrien, look for the resume speed sign. 3.1 miles later there is a right turn, travel a couple of hundred yards and you will see a sign for the house.

ANNESTOWN HOUSE

John & Pippa Galloway
Annestown
County Waterford
Tel: (051) 396160 Fax: 396474
relax@annestown.com
www.annestown.com

Annestown is the precious nugget on the gorgeous Copper Coast, one of the most beautiful, unspoilt and lonely strips of coastline in Ireland.

The Copper Coast, as the strip of coastline between Dungarvan and Tramore in County Waterford is known, is one of the most elemental, beautiful, and undiscovered parts of Ireland. How it has remained so undetected is something for which we should all give grateful thanks. And, maybe the nicest way to give thanks is to pay the Copper Coast the compliment of a visit, in which case you will have the added joy of encountering another elemental, understated little gem, John and Pippa Galloway's Annestown House, hard on the hill in the village. The Galloways are pioneering people: they opened Annestown as a dedicated restaurant - probably the first in Waterford - way back in 1977, and their considerable professional experience gives Annestown its just-right air of quiet confidence, making it the golden nugget in the Copper Coast, the perfect place to stay on the coast.

- **OPEN:** mid Mar-end Oct
- **ROOMS:** Five rooms, all double or twin
- **PRICE:** €50-€70 per person sharing, B&B

- **NOTES:**
Amex, Visa, Mastercard accepted. Dinner, €33, 7.45pm Mon-Sat, book by previous bedtime. Individual tables. No wheelchair access. Partially enclosed parking. Children welcome, cot, high chair.

- **DIRECTIONS:**
6 miles west of Tramore on R675. 12 miles from Waterford, 16 miles from Dungarvan. Signpost from Tramore.

BUGGY'S GLENCAIRN INN

Ken & Cathleen Buggy
Glencairn, nr Lismore
County Waterford
Tel & Fax: (058) 56232
buggysglencairninn@eircom.net
www.buggys.net

Forget Tracey Emin's bed:
Ken and Cathleen Buggy's
beds in the Glencairn Inn are
the Rembrandts of repose.

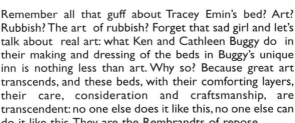

Remember all that guff about Tracey Emin's bed? Art? Rubbish? The art of rubbish? Forget that sad girl and let's talk about real art: what Ken and Cathleen Buggy do in their making and dressing of the beds in Buggy's unique inn is nothing less than art. Why so? Because great art transcends, and these beds, with their comforting layers, their care, consideration and craftsmanship, are transcendent: no one else does it like this, no one else can do it like this. They are the Rembrandts of repose.

But the Buggy's artistry extends to every element of the Glencairn Inn, from the bountiful breakfasts to the blissful comfort of the bar, from beautiful dinners with Mr Buggy's signature fish cookery to a calm, endless hospitality which you will never forget. This is truly hospitality as an art form, instinct and application fused into a concept that is wholly original, wholly unique.

- **OPEN:** Jan-end Nov
- **ROOMS:** Five rooms, all en suite
- **PRICE:** €110 per room, B&B

- **NOTES:**
Dinner from 7.30pm-9pm, booking essential €35
Secure car parking.
No wheelchair access. No facilities for very young children.

- **DIRECTIONS:**
In Lismore turn right at the monument, go to Horneybrook's garage, there is a sign to Glencairn. Follow this road for 3 miles, until you come to the Inn.

GORTNADIHA

Eileen & Tom Harty
Ring, Dungarvan
County Waterford
Tel: (058) 46142
ringcheese@eircom.net
waterfordfarms.com/gortnadiha

Former artisan cheesemaker Eileen
Harty revels in the vocation of
keeping a lovely B&B in Gortnadiha:
the lady has found her new groove.

Having long been one of the great farmhouse
cheesemakers, Eileen Harty has re-invented herself as
one of the great B&B keepers. There is no mystery as to
how she should have been able to switch careers so
seamlessly: she is a sociable woman, a great hostess, and
her métier is sharing: sharing her lovely house, sharing
her food, right down to sharing information about
excellent new places to stay that she has encountered,
places that sing with the tenor of high standards that
drive women like Mrs Harty to do their very best.
And high standards is what Gortnadiha House is all
about. It's a high, handsome farmhouse on the hill as you
ascend towards the summit of Ring, and the rooms are
calm and comfortable, the breakfast a veritable
panjandrum of choice things. And Mrs Harty's sociable
nature brings the whole charming escapade all together.

- **OPEN:** 1 Feb-1 Dec
- **ROOMS:** Three rooms, all en suite
- **PRICE:** €30-40 per person sharing

- **NOTES:**
No dinner. No wheelchair access.
Children welcome. Visa, Mastercard accepted. Private
parking.

- **DIRECTIONS:**
Follow the curve of Dungarvan Bay. Come off the N25
at the junction for Ring (3km from Dungarvan).
Signposted from here. Midway between Waterford and
Cork. 2 hours from Rosslare.

HANORA'S COTTAGE

Seamus & Mary Wall
Nire Valley, nr Clonmel
County Waterford
Tel: (052) 36134, Fax: 36540
hanorascottage@eircom.net
www.hanorascottage.com

The Wall family are the West Waterford pioneers, folk who created the template which has made the region a success.

They are the true West Waterford pioneers, the Wall family. Now that this glorious region has become quietly renowned for great food and great hospitality, we should remember that Seamus and Mary Wall were here long before anyone else, establishing the sort of standards in Hanora's which others, who have come along later, have had to emulate in order to become successful. Blessed be those who create the template, for that is what the Wall family have done with their food, their hospitality, their joie de vivre. West Waterford needs them.

The part of the template which no others can emulate is, of course, their staggeringly brilliant breakfasts, a feast which is surely the best in the country. It is just the tonic to get you out walking in the hills of the beautiful Nire Valley, with the consolation of Eoin Wall's cooking in the restaurant to bring the day to a beautiful conclusion.

- **OPEN:** All year, except Christmas
- **ROOMS:** 10 rooms
- **PRICE:** €75-€85 per person sharing. Single occupancy of double room €80-€100. Room 5, €125

- **NOTES:**
Restaurant open 6.30pm-9pm, €40.
Wheelchair access.
No children.
Secure parking.

- **DIRECTIONS:**
From Clonmel or Dungarvan, follow signs to Ballymaclery village. The house is signposted from there.

POWERSFIELD HOUSE

Eunice Power & Edmund Power
Ballinamuck West, Dungarvan
County Waterford
Tel: (058) 45594, Fax: 45550
powersfieldhouse@cablesurf.com
www.powersfield.com

Eunice Power is blessed with the
ability to do it all, it seems. Super
house, super cook, super woman.
Super-super-super-duper, says you.

Psychologists and general practitioners spend a lot of
time telling us that 'you can't do it all, you know'.
No one seems to have told Eunice Power.
Mrs Power does seem able to do it all. It would be
enough if she simply ran this lovely house and cooked
breakfast – superb breakfasts – for her guests. But, no, she
also likes to open her tiny dining room to guests and the
public at weekends when she shows that her cookery
skills are just as great as her skills at homemaking and
hospitality. Indeed, the last dinner we ate in Powersfield
was nothing less than a triumph, a superb demonstration
of cooking that unified comforting domestic flavours with
a professional élan that sent us singing into the night.
So, ordinary mortals such as ourselves can't do it all, but
Eunice Power can. More power to her motivation, for it
makes Powersfield House a thrilling, fab new address.

● **OPEN:** All year, except Christmas and New Year
● **ROOMS:** Six rooms, all en suite
● **PRICE:** €40-€45 p.p.s. Single room €50

● **NOTES:**
Amex, Visa, Mastercard, Laser. Dinner served Thu-Sat
and bank hol Sun, 7pm-9.30pm,
Full wheelchair access.
Children welcome.

● **DIRECTIONS:**
Take the Clonmel/Cappoquin road from Dungarvan, and
the house is the second turn to the left, and the first
house on the right.

RICHMOND HOUSE

Paul & Claire Deevy
Cappoquin
County Waterford
Tel: (058) 54278, Fax: 54988
info@richmondhouse.net
www.richmondhouse.net

Richmond is a modest, relaxed and relaxing country house, with dazzling cooking from Paul Deevy.

Ask yourself: why does Richmond House succeed? The answer, we would propose, is because it conforms to our dream of what a weekend escape should be like, should you want to get away to the country for a few days. It's not grand: it's comfortable. It's not lavish; it's understated. It doesn't feel like a professional country house; it feels more like a private house where you are a friend of the owners. Welcome.

All of these things mean that one feels superbly relaxed in Richmond: that is its essence: comfortable, calm, courtly, charming, chill-out.

All this would be enough on its own, but Claire Deevy's skills at f-o-h and Mr Deevy's brilliant cooking send everything at Richmond skywards into sheer bliss. This is amongst the most appropriate and delicious country cooking you can enjoy, in one of the best houses.

- **OPEN:** 20 Jan-20 Dec
- **ROOMS:** Nine rooms
- **PRICE:** from €60 p.p.s. Single supplement €20

- **NOTES:**
Restaurant open for dinner only, Mon-Sun (closed on Sun in winter), €45.
Recommended for special diets with advance notice.
No wheelchair access.
Private parking.
Children welcome, babysitting, cots, toys.

- **DIRECTIONS:**
Just outside Cappoquin, the house is well signposted.

TEMPLE COUNTRY HOUSE & HEALTH SPA

Declan & Bernadette Fagan
Horseleap, Moate
County Westmeath
Tel: (0506) 35118, Fax: 35008
info@templespa.ie
www.templespa.ie

north
east
west
south

Everyone is spending money on spas like crazy: they will need to do more than just spend money to catch up with the fine luxury of Temple Spa.

A spa is a place where there is a curative mineral spring. We don't know if Declan and Bernadette Fagan's house actually has a curative mineral spring, but we do know that Temple is an unparalleled fount of curative goodness. And this curative power is not just thanks to the fab, I-so-need-this treatments which the therapists offer for guests, though those treatments are sublime and reviving. Instead, the curative powers extend right down to the cooking and hospitality of the Fagans themselves. Mrs Fagan has always struck us as someone who has a profound gift for looking after people, for understanding what they need even before they recognise it themselves. Her cooking, then, is a vital part of the whole concept of Temple as a spa; this is food to recharge your batteries and your soul, great cooking that is light, energising, fantastic. You deserve Temple Spa, know that?

- **OPEN:** All year, except Christmas
- **ROOMS:** Eight rooms, all en suite
- **PRICE:** €205 p.p.s. for 24 hours midweek, Single €225. €375 p.p.s. Fri-Sun, €415 single. Three days midweek from €525 p.p.s., €575 single. All inclusive rates only.

- **NOTES:**
Mastercard, Visa, Amex accepted. Dinner, 8pm. Inclusive rates only. No wheelchair access. Children over 16 years welcome.

- **DIRECTIONS:**
Half a mile off the N6 Dublin-Galway road, and clearly signposted just after Horseleap, heading westwards.

WINEPORT LODGE

Jane English & Ray Byrne
Glasson, Athlone
County Westmeath
Tel: (0902) 85466, Fax: 85471
lodge@wineport.ie
www.wineport.ie

Wineport Lodge has been a true cult destination since it opened its doors. Great rooms, comfort and views add up to an ideal getaway for Dubliners.

Having breakfast on the verandah at Wineport Lodge, gazing out across the Lough, with ducks quacking, the little jetty bobbing, and with peace dropping slowly all around you, is some sort of bliss. When the verandahs are more perfectly sealed off one from the other – and you can have your breakfast in your birthday suit! – it will be more bliss that most of us can handle.

The Lodge has been developed smartly and organically from this fine, busy restaurant. The beds in the rooms face out towards the water, a brilliant piece of design which makes it seem – with a little imagination – as if you yourself could float out over the water. Superb furnishings make these true capsules of pleasure, and the public area is splendid. For stressed Dubliners, this is a perfect getaway, though we would like to see the restaurant step up a gear, completing the Wineport gig.

- **OPEN:** All year
- **ROOMS:** 10 rooms
- **PRICE:** €200-€275 double room rate, Single occupancy, Sun-Thu €150, Fri-Sat €200-€275

- **NOTES:**
All major cards accepted. Restaurant serves dinner, Value menu @ €30 for two courses, a la carte menu approx €45. Full wheelchair access.

- **DIRECTIONS:**
Take the Longford/Cavan exit off the Dublin/Galway road, fork left at the Dog and Duck pub, the Wineport Lodge is 1 mile further on on the left hand side.

CHURCHTOWN HOUSE

Patricia & Austin Coady
Tagoat, Rosslare
County Wexford
Tel: (053) 32555, Fax: 32577
info@churchtownhouse.com
www.churchtownhouse.com

The anniversaries are descending on Churchtown House in 2003: 300 birthdays for the house, and ten years since the Coadys began.

Churchtown is a very elegant, handsome house, set in acres of beautiful grounds just on the edge of Rosslare, and not too far from the main road, which makes this some sort of a dream first-night, last-night destination for ferry travellers: this really is as convenient as it gets, and the fact that the Coadys offer dinner in their pretty dining room is even more of a bonus for ship-weary travellers. Comfort is solid and understated in this superbly-maintained house, and whilst from the outside it might look like a real top-dollar place, prices are actually extremely fair, both for food and accommodation. The house will be celebrating its three hundredth anniversary this year, and the Coadys themselves will be celebrating a decade of taking guests, a decade which has seen their hospitality and good cooking gain a dedicated audience.

- **OPEN:** Early Mar-end Nov
- **ROOMS:** 12 rooms
- **PRICE:** €55-€110 per person sharing, Single supplement €15-€20
Rates available for B&B & dinner

- **NOTES:**
Visa, Mastercard, Amex. Dinner, €39, book by noon.
Not suitable for children under 10 years.
Wheelchair access.

- **DIRECTIONS:**
Five minutes' drive from Rosslare harbour. Turn off the N25 onto the R736 at Tagoat.

KELLY'S RESORT HOTEL

Bill Kelly
Rosslare
County Wexford
Tel: (053) 32114, Fax: 32222
kellyhot@iol.ie
www.kellys.ie

Character. And characters.
That's how you can define
the inimitable, extraordinary
Kelly's Resort Hotel.

Character. And characters. That's what Kelly's has got, in spades. Just think of the characters: Tom and Josie. Sheelagh and her team at the desk. Jim Aherne in the kitchen. Pat and Eddie in the dining room. Bill Kelly himself, quietly keeping this great big shop floating along, working just as hard as everyone else, and boy but this big crew work hard in Kelly's. Remarkable people, larger than life, unforgettable, folk you are delighted to see again,

And the character, that ennobling, distinguished and yet utterly democratic spirit which pervades the hotel, and which means high-rollers and hopefuls are equally at their ease, enjoying the delicious cooking, the extraordinary wines, the peerless collection of modern Irish art which is deftly added to each season. Like Ballymaloe House and a small number of other Irish addresses, Kelly's is a national treasure, an extraordinary icon of Irish culture.

- **OPEN:** Late Feb-early Dec
- **ROOMS:** 99 rooms, all en suite
- **PRICE:** Accommodation is quoted on a two-day, five-day or seven-day basis, full board.
See their website or telephone for appropriate rates

- **NOTES:**
Lunch and Dinner served in their restaurant. All rates include full board. La Marine restaurant also open and comes recommended. Full wheelchair access.
Children welcome, every facility for babies and children.

- **DIRECTIONS:**
Clearly signposted in Rosslare and from the main road.

McMENAMIN'S TOWNHOUSE

Seamus & Kay McMenamin
3 Auburn Terrace
Redmond Road, Wexford
County Wexford
Tel: (053) 46442
mcmem@indigo.ie
www.wexford-bedandbreakfast.com

McMenamin's continues to offer one of the very best breakfasts, cooked with care, and served with panache and true hospitality.

So, what did your aunt and uncle think of the breakfast? 'Excellent. Plenty of choice and quality universally good. All served with tremendous panache. 'Specially remembered: porridge with rum 'halo' and superb devilled kidneys.' Thanks for that.

My goodness, but some porridge with a halo of rum and some devilled kidneys would be just the ticket any morning of the week, wouldn't it? Supplying travellers with just this sort of morning time rocket fuel, and doing it with such panache, is just what Seamus and Kay McMenamin have always done so well: the McMenamin's breakfast is one of the best. The breakfast remains benchmark, but we would like to see some redecoration of the rooms, which are beginning to show a little age. Do note that whilst the house is very handy for Wexford town, it is also convenient for the ferries at Rosslare.

- **OPEN:** All year, except Christmas
- **ROOMS:** Five rooms, all en suite
- **PRICE:** €45 per person sharing. Single €50

- **NOTES:**
No dinner.
No wheelchair access.
Locked parking.
Children welcome, high chair, cot, babysitting.

- **DIRECTIONS:**
In the centre of Wexford, directly opposite the bus and railway stations. Beside the large Dunnes Stores supermarket.

10 GREAT
NEW DISCOVERIES

AN BOHREEN
DUNGARVAN, Co. WATERFORD

ANNA'S HOUSE
COMBER, Co. DOWN

BALLYKNOCKEN HOUSE
ASHFORD, Co. WICKLOW

COXTOWN MANOR
LAGHEY, Co. DONEGAL

MARBLE HALL
DONNYBROOK, Co. DUBLIN

MOY HOUSE
LAHINCH, Co. CLARE

OTTO'S CREATIVE CATERING
BUTLERSTOWN, Co. CORK

ROCK COTTAGE
SCHULL, Co. CORK

TODDIES
KINSALE, Co. CORK

WINEPORT LODGE
ATHLONE, Co. WESTMEATH

SALVILLE HOUSE

Jane & Gordon Parker
Salville, Enniscorthy
County Wexford
Tel: (054) 35252, Fax 35252
info@salvillehouse.com
www.salvillehouse.com

Salville is a magical house, a place that gives you everything you could ever want, in exactly the way you want it. *icon*

What we love about Salville is the quiet understatement of everything in the house – the design, the style, the furnishings, the way in which the house is allowed to be itself – and the quiet excellence which drives Gordon and Jane Parker to do their very best. You cannot be as good as this couple are at their job – and they are amongst the very best hosts and cooks – without having a very clear idea of exactly what you want to do and exactly how you want to do it. They know what they want.

Put this understatement and this ambition together, and you get something special indeed, a place where every detail is crafted with the precision of artists at work. Mr Parker's cooking has won huge critical acclaim, and it is worthy of every piece of praise. Not only is it superb cooking, it is also superb value for money. Salville quite simply gives you everything you could possibly want.

● **OPEN:** All year, except Christmas
● **ROOMS:** Five rooms. One two-bedroom self-contained apartment available for B&B or self catering
● **PRICE:** €40 per person sharing

● **NOTES:**
Dinner, 8pm, €30. No wheelchair access. Secure parking. Children welcome. This year sees renovation of tennis court. Croquet and boules also available.

● **DIRECTIONS:**
Just off the N11 to Wexford - take the first left after the hospital, go up the hill to a T-junction then turn left and proceed for half km.

BALLYKNOCKEN HOUSE

Catherine Fulvio
Gleanealy, Ashford
County Wicklow
Tel: (0404) 44627, Fax: 44696
cfulvio@ballyknocken.com
www.ballyknocken.com

north

east

west

south

Brilliant cooking, especially of superb local meats, is just one secret of Catherine Fulvio's rather super house.

One of the nicest things we have eaten in a very long time was the roasted fillet of pork, stuffed with sage, apple and onion, which Catherine Fulvio cooked for us one evening in lovely Ballyknocken. Peerless meat met peerless cookery in an embrace of the utterly delicious. The fact that the soup – turnip and brown bread soup with brown bread croutons – was fantastic, and that the vegetables were fantastic and that the chocolate amaretto cake was also fantastic had us thinking: this is fantastic!

And so it is. Ballyknocken is a gem, and Mrs Fulvio is a star: we would get this young woman her own telly show tomorrow, but sure who listens to us? Actually, we know that her work in Ballyknocken will make her famous, no doubt about that. It's a lovely house, dominated by Mrs Fulvio's truly sweet temperament, and if you need to be rescued, then this Wicklow hideaway is waiting for you.

- **OPEN:** Feb-Nov
- **ROOMS:** Seven rooms
- **PRICE:** From €45-€55 per person sharing. Single supplement €30

- **NOTES:**
Visa, Mastercard. Dinner, Mon-Sat, €28.
No wheelchair access.
Children welcome.

- **DIRECTIONS:**
From Dublin, head south to Ashford (on N11), then turn right after Chester Beatty pub. Continue for 3 miles and the house is on the right.

THE BROOK LODGE INN

Evan, Eoin & Bernard Doyle
Macreddin Village, Aughrim
County Wicklow
Tel: (0402) 36444, Fax: 36580
brooklodge@macreddin.ie
www.brooklodge.com

Even the potato crisps are handmade in the Brook Lodge, proof of Evan Doyle's meticulous attention to detail in this admirable country hotel.

From the outside, it's a bit sterile and contrived: this new 'old' village complex with its pub, corner store, quaint chapel, and rather ordinary-looking hotel. But a closer look, and a stay, dispels any notion of cuteness or kitsch. Instead, owner Evan Doyle has appropriated all the best qualities of Europe's and Ireland's finest country house hotels with his own vision for an ecologically sustainable environment, providing an understated graciousness and luxury of the highest order. The guest rooms, done in country style, are nothing remarkable, but they are very comfortable. Where Brook Lodge shines is in its easy, spacious public rooms with their white terracotta-tiled floors, thick carpets, big open fireplaces, two strategically placed bars, and to-die-for comfortable sofas. Evan Doyle's attention to detail is notable in everything from Brook Lodge's homemade crisps to the superb service.

- **OPEN:** All year, including Christmas
- **ROOMS:** 55 rooms and suites
- **PRICE:** €87.50-135 per person sharing, single supplements apply. Rates for B&B & Dinner (check web)

- **NOTES:**
All major cards accepted. Restaurant, pubs, market and bakery, dinner €48. Secure car parking. Reservations essential. No wheelchair access. Children welcome.

- **DIRECTIONS:**
N11 Dublin to Rathnew, Co Wicklow. Right at r'about, on to Gleneally, on to Rathdrum. 1 mile outside Rathdrum, right towards Aughrim via Ballinaclash.

NORTHERN IRELAND

ANNA'S HOUSE

Anna Johnson
Tullynagee, 35 Lisbarnett Rd
Comber, County Down
Tel: 024 9754 1566
anna@annashouse.info
www.annashouse.info

Anna's House is an enchantment: an extraordinary garden, incredibly sophisticated food from a true cook, and a simply incredible experience.

Be careful: Anna and Ken Johnson's house has the ability to mesmerise. 'Enchanted, whimsical, semi-wild wonderland'; 'exceptional experience'; 'brought back all my childhood imaginings of the Secret Garden'; 'Anna's food sparkles with the vitality, intelligence, and passion that underlie her modesty'.

Blimey! Whatever happened to the hard-bitten, seen-it-all, eaten-it-all critics from the Bridgestone Guides? Missing, presumed lost in the mists of reverie and deliciousness that this special house and garden enfold you in. But then, who could resist a delicate, cream-laced lettuce soup, or pale-pink salmon with garden vegetables, or a sweet apple and custard crumble? Who wouldn't swoon over Ken's still-cooling bloomer loaf with garden strawberry jam, or a dill and parsley omelette, then some of Anna's squidgy-soft scones. Then, a walk in the incredible garden, and a chance to dream.

- **OPEN:** All year, except Christmas
- **ROOMS:** 3 rooms
- **PRICE:** stg£25 per person

- **NOTES:**
Dinner by request, stg£15-£20. Secure car parking. No wheelchair access. Babies in arms welcome, but not suitable for children.

- **DIRECTIONS:**
In Lisbane pass the petrol station, turn right into Lisbarnett Road. After exactly 0.6 miles and just after a right hand bend you will see on the right a private concrete lane leading straight up a hill. Follow this lane.

ASH ROWAN

Evelyn & Sam Hazlett
12 Windsor Avenue
Belfast, County Antrim
Tel: (028) 9066 1758
Fax: 9066 3227
ashrowan@hotmail.com

Extraordinary, amazing breakfasts are a centrepiece of the lovely Ash Rowan, a place of endless, caring hospitality.

'We take great care about our breakfast and we want you to write about it!' So say Sam and Evelyn Hazlett, and, boy, but they do take care with the cooking, offering everything from the archetypal Ulster Fry, that glorious concoction with both soda farls and potato bread, along with tipsy porridge – a shot of Drambuie and cream to get you motoring at breakneck speed - and there are great Edwardian staples such as kedgeree, and a fresh fish of the day which is pan-fried in herb flavoured butter. But, don't forget the house special of mushrooms flambéed in sherry with some cream, or the Irish Scramble which mixes three (3!) eggs with bacon, mushrooms and a little grated cheese. Vegetarians are properly looked after, and Continentals can get a Continental breakfast, if they are crazy enough. It's bounteous, and it's typical of the generosity that is part and parcel of lovely Ash Rowan.

- **OPEN:** All year, except Christmas
- **ROOMS:** Six rooms, all en suite
- **PRICE:** from stg£66 per person sharing, stg£48 single

- **NOTES:**
Dinner 7pm, stg£28, separate tables. Reservation essential, 24 hours' notice required.
Locked car parking. No wheelchair access. Children over 12 years welcome.

- **DIRECTIONS:**
Go through Bradbury Place on to University Road. Windsor Avenue is the 3rd Avenue on the right past the Botanic Inn.

BEECH HILL COUNTRY HOUSE

north
east
west
south

Victoria Brann
23 Ballymoney Road
Craigantlet, County Down
Tel: (028) 9042 5892
info@beech-hill.net
www.beech-hill.net

Professionalism and comfort are the keynotes of Victoria Brann's elegant, stylish house.

comfy

Beech Hill has a handsome timelessness about it. You would hardly believe, looking at this confident, one-and-a-half storey house, that it was already more than 40 years old, for it looks so contemporary, so modern, so unusual for Northern Ireland, where suburbia and Victorianism tend to do battle, with little or nothing in between.

Victoria Brann has the right sort of confident stylist's eye to suit the house, and the interiors are decorated just right: restrained, colourful, concordant, everything summoning up a deeply pleasing comfort. She is an exacting hostess, is Ms Brann, someone in whom 25 years of working as a Cordon Bleu-trained chef shows in every detail of her work, and yet she throws off all her hard work with a shrug, as if it was little or nothing. It's actually very hard work, but she is supremely confident and able, and it's a treat to watch someone so capable.

- **OPEN:** All year
- **ROOMS:** Three rooms
- **PRICE:** stg£64 for double room, £42 single

- **NOTES:**
Mastercard, Visa. No dinner.
Wheelchair access with assistance. Secure parking.
Children over 12 years only.

- **DIRECTIONS:**
15 minutes from Belfast city airport. Leave Belfast on the A2. Bypass Holywood. 1.5 miles from bridge at Ulster Folk Museum, turn right Ballymoney road, signed to Craigantlet. House is 1.75 miles on left.

MADDYBENNY FARMHOUSE

Rosemary White
Portrush
County Antrim
Tel: (028) 70823394, Fax: 70822177
accommodation@
maddybenny22.freeserve.co.uk

Flower-festooned, hospitable, and home to one of the mightiest breakfasts known to mankind, Maddybenny is a great B&B.

Rosemary White is one of the archetypal figures of Northern Irish hospitality, and whilst Maddybenny has developed steadily over the years, and now includes a fleet of six self-catering cottages on the farm and a serious horse riding school, Mrs White remains famous first and foremost for her hospitality, and also for her extraordinary breakfasts, gargantuan feasts for which she has deservedly won every award imaginable.

Everything you could desire is on offer, from American waffles to porridge necklaced with Drambuie or Irish Mist, from kippers with lemon and dill to smoked trout ramekin, and then any and every version of the classic Ulster Fry, with either a modest collation of ingredients or the whole works, depending on your appetite. The rooms are thoughtful and cosy: after that breakfast you might find it hard to resist returning to them for a snooze.

- **OPEN:** Jan-Nov inclusive
- **ROOMS:** Two family rooms, one double, one single
- **PRICE:** stg£25-£27.50 per person (They will also accept euros at €40/£25)

- **NOTES:**
Visa, Mastercard accepted. No meals. No wheelchair access. Secure parking. Children welcome, all facilities for babies. Six self-catering cottages available. Riding centre, and very 'golfer friendly'.

- **DIRECTIONS:**
50 miles from Belfast, signposted off the A29 Portrush/Coleraine.

THE MOAT INN

Robert & Rachel Thompson
12 Donegore Hill
Templepatrick
County Antrim
Tel: (028) 9443 3659 Fax: 9443 3726
themoatinn@talk21.com

Style lovers and food lovers will both be in their element in the Thompsons' Moat Inn.

'Although we always stress that we are not a restaurant, the Belfast Telegraph gave us a favourable restaurant review...' Well, if style lovers have always cherished The Moat Inn as an oasis of idiosyncratic style and good taste, it was only a matter of time before the food lovers got in with their own good taste and sent forward the word about Rachel Thompson's splendid cooking. And what cooking: confit of duck with sweet spiced lentils; onion tart with honey and orange dressing; tomato and harissa soup; char-grilled seabass with oriental ginger dressing and toasted sesame seeds; pecan and pistachio filo layer with maple syrup and vanilla cream. This is serious cooking, worthy of anyone's accolades, and it attracts locals who can now eat here in private parties, as well as the happy guests. Style and cooking elide seamlessly together in The Moat, making for a special place indeed.

- **OPEN:** Open all year
- **ROOMS:** Two double rooms, one twin, all en suite
- **PRICE:** stg£30-£35 per person, B&B

- **NOTES:**
Visa, Mastercard, Switch. Dinner 8pm (book by noon) stg£22.50. No wheelchair access.
Secure parking.
Children welcome, cots and babysitting.

- **DIRECTIONS:**
From Belfast, take M2 to Templepatrick. At roundabout, follow brown signs to Donegore. Moat Inn is a blue house on Donegore Hill below the garden centre.

STRANGFORD COTTAGE

Maureen Thornton
Castle Street, Strangford
County Down
Tel: (028) 4488 1208
Fax: 4488 1256
m.e.thornton@o2.co.uk

Strangford Cottage is picture-postcard-pretty, and animated by Maureen Thornton's eager energy: a truly delightful destination.

It's more than a bit embarrassing to look back at the notes you make doing Bridgestone visits, sometimes. Take the notes made when at Strangford Cottage: 'lovely old Wellstode in the kitchen'; 'lovely bath in the centre of the bathroom'; 'lovely sitting room'; 'lovely garden room'; 'lovely striped wallpaper in landing'. Oh dear. Still it could have been worse: we could have said 'nice' rather than the endless 'lovely'.

But, lovely is what Maureen Thornton's house truly is. It may be 200 years old, but it has the colourful charm and chutzpah of a very contemporary space, and the hostess herself animates the house with a theatrical energy that is completely winning. Indeed, our notes conclude with the observation that the rooms 'are like theatre sets; each is accurately and precisely pitched'. So, head down to Strangford and enjoy the drama of the house yourself.

- **OPEN:** Apr-Sep
- **ROOMS:** Three double rooms
- **PRICE:** stg£45-£60 per person sharing. Single supplement stg£20

- **NOTES:**
No credit cards accepted. Afternoon tea.
No wheelchair access.
Secure parking in front of house.

- **DIRECTIONS:**
30 miles from Belfast. Newry - take Hilltown rd to Downpatrick. Belfast - take Newcastle signpost to Carryduff. Follow signpost from Downpatrick.

INDEX

'For the native it might be a shock to discover the riches that abound here. For the visitor, for whom there is no other way to discover the best places to eat and shop for food, the Bridgestone Food Lover's Guide to Northern Ireland is, quite simply, indispensable.'

SETH LINDER
THE IRISH NEWS

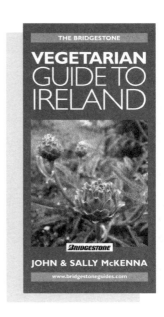

'An invaluable gourmet reference for both round-the-country ramblings and sourcing the best grub in your home town... packed with great information on local markets, producers and pubs with grub.'

LOUISE EAST
THE IRISH TIMES

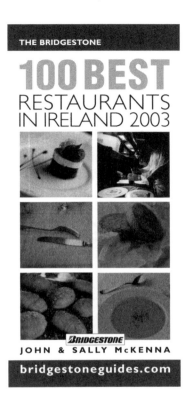

THE BRIDGESTONE

100 BEST
RESTAURANTS IN IRELAND 2003

JOHN & SALLY McKENNA

bridgestoneguides.com

The companion volume to this guide is...

The Bridgestone
100 BEST RESTAURANTS IN IRELAND 2003

• The hottest new openings, the hippest city destinations, the most romantic country getaways.

• This is the guide that tells you the who, what and where of Ireland's contemporary culinary culture.

The Bridgestone Guides...
ON THE WEB

To access up-to-the-minute information about Ireland's food culture, and to discover any changes or alterations that may have occurred with the entries in the Bridgestone guides visit:

www.bridgestoneguides.com